Heart
of the
Problem

When you're tired
of "just coping"
with your struggles
and want to
find a cure,
you're ready to
face the

Heart
of the
Problem

Henry Brandt & Kerry L. Skinner
Foreword by Henry T. Blackaby

BROADMAN
&HOLMAN
PUBLISHERS

Nashville, Tennessee

4260-60
0-8054-6060-8

Published by
Broadman & Holman Publishers, Nashville, Tennessee
Acquisitions and Development Editor: John Landers
Page Design: Desktop Miracles, Addison, Texas

Dewey Decimal Classification: 153.4
Subject Heading: PROBLEM SOLVING—
RELIGIOUS LIFE / CHRISTIAN LIFE
Library of Congress Card Catalog Number: 96-33389

Library of Congress Cataloging-in-Publication Data
Brandt, Henry R.
     The heart of the problem : how to stop coping and find the cure for life's struggles / Henry Brandt, Kerry L. Skinner.
          p. cm.
     Includes bibliographical references and indexes.
     ISBN 0-8054-6060-8
     1. Christian life—Baptist authors.   I. Skinner, Kerry L.,
II. Title.
BV4501.2.B6858   1997
248.4'861—dc20   96-33389
                                                              CIP

97 98 99 00 01 1 2 3 4 5

From Henry Brandt

To Eva . . .
> you are in heaven.
> For forty-two years,
> we forged biblical principles
> that have stood the test of time.

To Marcey . . .
> my second wife in heaven also.
> For three delightful years,
> we applied many of the same principles.

To Jo . . .
> my third wife.
> Now married nine years.
> A widow for twelve years;
> we needed each other.
> Together, we travel the world
> teaching biblical lessons
> and watching new life spring up.

From Kerry L. Skinner

To Elaine . . .
> My wife of twenty-three years,
> who has walked with me in giving
> our lives to teach others how to
> walk in the ways of Christ.

To Jason . . .
> my son who is an inspiration
> to me by how he loves his Lord and
> his wife Christa.

To God be the glory for how He has called
many people to help teach me so that in
turn I may "teach others also."
(2 Tim. 2:2)

CONTENTS

FOREWORD

There comes to every child of God, and to every person, a wonderful word from God. It touches the deepest needs in the human experience—peace in the heart and in the entire life.

May the God of peace . . .
equip you with everything good for doing his will,
and may he work in us what is pleasing to him,
through Jesus Christ,
to whom be glory for ever and ever.
HEBREWS 13:20–21, NIV

Dr. Brandt has done a great service to the earnest, seeking heart by doing two things:

1. Confronting us with ourselves, often at our most difficult and bewildering moments;
2. Confronting us with God's clear provision for our every condition.

He deals with tenderness yet transparent truthfulness in regard to several of the most significant factors in our lives:

peace, joy, anger, bitterness, crises, forgiveness, sin, honesty, and interpersonal relationships.

In doing so, Dr. Brandt returns us again and again to the only places to which we can turn: God, His Word (the Bible), the Holy Spirit, prayer, and faith.

The world, and even well-meaning Christians, will give counsel that is not from God. What kind of response should there be? There should be a clear and resounding turning to God through the Scriptures and a confident trust in Him.

There is no doubt that Dr. Brandt has tested and proved God's ways and faithful provision in his own life! Sharing out of the depths of his own crises, his time with missionaries, and the tender moments with those who have sought his counsel, he brings light and affirmation from real life to the counsels of God. He shares the Scriptures and shows from real life experiences how faithful God is to those whose hearts are right with Him.

We have too much of the "world's counsel and reasoning" as a substitute for God's counsel and truth. Dr. Brandt presents a refreshing and much needed "return to God!"

Much practical help is gained from the pastoral experiences of Kerry L. Skinner. His years as an associate pastor and minister of education, guiding God's people into daily relationships with Jesus Christ, add much to the personalizing of life the truths given by Dr. Brandt.

This material can be missed if read without thinking. Great truths, presented in clear, simple language and illustrations, can be overlooked. Read it slowly and thoughtfully! Pause, reflect, and meditate on each day's thoughts. Then faithfully seek the enabling of God's Spirit to bring you to God's fullness in Jesus Christ. Live life as Jesus promised, in His peace and His joy!

"As the Father has loved me,
so have I loved you.
Now remain in my love.
If you obey my commands,
you will remain in my love,
just as I have obeyed my Father's commands
and remain in his love.
I have told you this
so that my joy may be in you and
that your joy may be complete.—

JOHN 15:9–11, NIV

This book is quite timely for our day! May God use Dr. Brandt's faithful witness and earnest pleas to return to God on His revealed terms as an instrument for revival among His people and spiritual awakening in our land.

—HENRY T. BLACKABY

INTRODUCTION

I have observed that individuals who move effectively through the ups and downs of life are regular church-goers. The weekly sermon, the Sunday school program, the music program, the educational program, and Christian fellowship all help. Consistent partaking of such helps and practicing the teaching will provide the strength for each day.

However, many regular church-goers enter into difficult situations in life. The major question to answer will be whether the situation makes us respond a certain way or whether the situation *will reveal* what is in the heart.

Jesus said,

> **"What comes out of a man,
> that defiles a man."**
> MARK 7:20

According to Jesus, what comes out of our mouths, or our lives, comes from the depths of our hearts. Do you really know what is in your heart? God always knows.

While God knows our hearts, it is important we know His heart. As you make your way through this book you will gradually learn what is in God's heart. God says:

"For My thoughts are not your thoughts,
Nor are your ways My ways," says the LORD.
ISAIAH 55:8

My wife, Eva, and I planned to walk hand-in-hand through the 1980s. We had been married forty years and were looking forward to a peaceful passage serving God. Instead, after a long struggle with cancer, Eva was laid to rest. It was April 1982. About this time I learned that I had Parkinson's disease.

Marcy and I married in June 1983. She died suddenly in August 1986.

Jo and I have been married since July 1987. A widow for twelve years, God had been preparing her to walk side by side with me. We have been serving God together, and He has led us along pleasant paths.

The anticipated peaceful path through the 1980s turned out to be a series of unbelievable and spectacular steep hills and valleys. I do not understand why God led me along that path. I learned that the Comforter whom Jesus said He would send to abide with us forever (John 14:16) was indeed with us.

One of my favorite Bible verses has given us understanding of our journey:

Oh, the depth of the riches
both of the wisdom and knowledge of God!
How unsearchable are His judgments
and His ways past finding out!
ROMANS 11:33

Acting on biblical principles results in lasting change and deepening fellowship with God. The Scripture states:

But if we walk in the light as He is in the light,
we have fellowship with one another,
and the blood of Jesus Christ His Son
cleanses us from all sin.
1 JOHN 1:7

Continuous exposure to biblical principles will also illustrate your allegiance to God:

"And you shall know the truth,
and the truth shall make you free."
JOHN 8:32

Jesus had an advantage in His approach to people:

◆ He knew their hearts. (Acts 15:8)
◆ He didn't need a case history.

Jesus knew that the heart of the problem was the problem of the heart. The decade of the 1980s has made another Bible verse come alive and is the theme of this book:

Keep your heart with all diligence,
for out of it spring the issues of life.
PROVERBS 4:23

As you make your way through this book, I hope you will join with multitudes of God's people saying:

He will teach us His ways,
and we shall walk in His paths.
ISAIAH 2:3

CHAPTER 1

The Myth of Complexity

Thought Starter

What do you say?
God is or God isn't?

♦

**But I fear, lest somehow,
as the serpent deceived Eve by his craftiness,
so your minds may be corrupted
from the simplicity that is in Christ.**
2 CORINTHIANS 11:3

Why Are So Many Christians Unhappy?

What I teach across the world is based on forty years of Bible memorization and reflection. Acting on these insights has been life-changing for me and my clients. My counseling career began in 1942 when, as a twenty-six-year-old engineer, the Holy Spirit tamed my vicious temper. People who knew me marveled at the change. Some of them asked if I could help them. With little knowledge of the Bible, my wife and I gathered verses useful for my friends and me. Two in particular caught my attention:

**Blessed is the man
who walks not in the counsel of the ungodly,
nor stands in the path of sinners,
nor sits in the seat of the scornful;
but his delight is in the law of the LORD,
And in His law he meditates day and night.**
PSALMS 1:1–2

**Great peace have those who love Your law,
and nothing causes them to stumble.**
PSALMS 119:165

2

To obey biblical guidelines as I lived out my life, I needed them in my head. For me, this clearly meant Bible memorization. Even now, fifty years later, I still consider Bible memorization and application is the single most important aid in my Christian life and in my counseling.

During the challenging years of obtaining a doctorate in clinical psychology, I listened to hundreds of stories from all levels of life and economic backgrounds. During those years, I studied with a secular textbook in one hand and a Bible in the other. I saw a wide gulf between the two approaches.

The benefits of Bible study are summed up in these Scriptures:

> For the word of God is living and powerful,
> and sharper than any two-edged sword,
> piercing even to the division of soul and spirit,
> and of joints and marrow,
> and is a discerner
> of the thoughts and intents of the heart.
>
> HEBREWS 4:12

> "Heaven and earth will pass away,
> but My words will by no means pass away."
>
> MATTHEW 24:35

> All Scripture is given by inspiration of God,
> and is profitable for doctrine, for reproof,
> for correction, for instruction in righteousness.
>
> 2 TIMOTHY 3:16

God's healing love can transform the most miserable life into one of comfort, joy, and deep personal peace. In the following pages take a look at the relief available through people helping people, through human efforts apart from God. Then explore the many dimensions of Christ, the Cure.

I recommend that you memorize the verse at the beginning of each chapter. Think about the verse for a week or two.

- Recall the verse as often as possible.
- Examine what the verse means to you.
- Discuss the verse with others.
- Observe yourself in relation to the verse.
- Compare the verse to what you hear on radio and TV, in conversations and sermons.
- Compare the verse to what you read in books, magazines, and newspapers.
- Find other Bible verses that are similar.

Ten verses in your head at the end of this book are much better than a hundred pages in your notebook. Don't rush.

Hopefully these lessons that I have collected from more than fifty-plus years of living will help you along your way. Remember, you have a choice: relief or cure.

God Is Able

In late 1947 I enrolled in graduate school and for the first time in my life I was taught by highly trained, thoughtful, dedicated professors who not only used textbooks that ruled out God but who themselves sincerely believed there is no God. For them, *God isn't.*

In my studies in clinical psychology we grappled with the challenge of helping disturbed people. We thoughtfully pondered how to help hostile, hateful, resentful, rebellious, frustrated, confused, angry, cruel, selfish, dishonest, and destructive people.

We all agreed that these words accurately described the dark side of human behavior. We were taught that a person is a biological organism whose total personality is the product of functioning in a social and cultural context.

We were also taught that a disturbed person is one whose needs are not met when he comes into the world, who is neglected, who lives in an environment that is cold and indifferent toward him. To understand what is behind this disturbed person's behavior is to seek complex origins in a murky past. The process can take months or years. Then the question is asked: What in the world can be changed or given to release this person from a prison of destructive emotions and behavior?

"No deity can save us. We must save ourselves."

This is the position taken in secular colleges, secular textbooks, in most graduate training, and in a formidable mass of "scientific research." This is the operating philosophy of government, heavily financed mental health agencies, professionally trained counselors, and the bulk of medically trained personnel.

Human problems are not ignored. In fact, we spend billions of dollars annually searching for solutions. Educators, politicians, psychiatrists, psychologists, sociologists, social workers, social agencies, and law enforcement agencies confront these problems every day.

A massive group of people—intelligent, educated, influential, politically powerful people—who have the best interests of humanity at heart, firmly and fiercely reject the concepts of sin, a creator, and a God. You might compare that host of people to a huge giant called Goliath. They firmly believe: *God isn't.*

Then there is another tiny group standing up to Goliath. This group (and I am one of them) believes that God *is.* We agree with the Goliath crowd that these words accurately describe the dark side of human behavior (hostile, hateful, resentful, rebellious, frustrated, confused, angry, cruel, selfish, dishonest, destructive).

At this point in the road, however, we come to a fork. We disagree that these words describing human behavior are socially and culturally caused. Our guidebook is the Bible. This book puts all those descriptive words under one heading. The heading is *Sin*.

In the Bible, Jesus commented on the nature of people:

> **And He said,**
> **"What comes out of a man, that defiles a man.**
> **For from within, out of the heart of men,**
> **proceed evil thoughts, adulteries, fornications, murders,**
> **thefts, covetousness, wickedness, deceit, licentiousness,**
> **an evil eye, blasphemy, pride, foolishness.**
> **All these evil things come from within and defile a man."**
> MARK 7:20–23

The apostle Paul gives us a description of our sinful nature.

> **Now the works of the flesh are evident, which are:**
> **adultery, fornication, uncleanness, licentiousness,**
> **idolatry, sorcery, hatred, contentions, jealousies,**
> **outbursts of wrath, selfish ambitions, dissensions,**
> **heresies, envy, murders, drunkenness,**
> **revelries, and the like.**
> GALATIANS 5:19–21

We are born with sinful hearts. Society only brings out of our hearts what is already there. When our Leader announced to the Goliath crowd that He came to save them from their sins, they replied with one thunderous voice: *Crucify Him.* They did.

In standing up to Goliath our little group might be compared to a little boy called David. We dare to use the word *sin* and affirm there is no human remedy for sin. You need a Savior who will cleanse you from sin and empower you to walk in the Spirit (in love, joy, peace, long-suffering, kindness, goodness, faithfulness, gentleness, and self-control).

If it is sin, that's good news. Sin is the simplest thing in the world to deal with. Jesus died to cleanse us from sin.

"Too simple," says the Goliath crowd.

Make no mistake. The people who approach life from humanistic assumptions make up a huge majority of the people you deal with every day. How long has it been since you had a conversation about sin and its cure?

You need to expand your knowledge of sin so that you know how Jesus can help you. This book will teach you how to live free from the bondage of sin and empower you to enjoy the fruit of the Spirit.

Jesus doesn't need a case history. He knows our hearts.

The Spirit's Life Is the Best Life

Once I came upon a hopeful statement:

For the LORD gives wisdom;
From His mouth come knowledge and understanding.
PROVERBS 2:6

I began to pray for wisdom and understanding. Over a period of months I experienced some amazing encounters and results with people seeking help. I can't claim credit because my input was often very minor.

Examine some of these experiences of people who have come to me with their burdens. You judge if these stories are too simple.

Tragic Deaths

He must have been in his early forties. She looked a bit younger. She held a little baby, perhaps two months old. They had anticipated this week-long family conference situated in a wooded area beside a clear, large lake.

Tragedy had marred the last year. Their four-year-old daughter had died after a lingering illness. During the next pregnancy, both their families gathered at the hospital for the results of an ultrasound test to determine the sex of their unborn second child. Expecting an exciting announcement, the whole family was shocked when a somber doctor stated that the baby she was carrying was dead.

It was a heavy Christmas that year. Very few of their friends stood with them. They faced their sorrow alone. Even the progress of a third pregnancy and their new son's birth had not eased their pain.

We were two days into the family conference. They were not enjoying themselves as they had hoped. The double deaths a year ago haunted them here with all the other families together in the dining room. He was also burdened with the recent failure of a business relationship which had left him with a large financial obligation.

Could I help them? He sat with clenched teeth behind tight lips. She held on to her little baby with a look of desperation.

How could anyone bear such trouble? No glib answer would magically remove their burdens.

I had to make a decision. The answer seemed clear to me. However, my guess was that they were not ready to talk about answers; they were too preoccupied with their problems. I encouraged and prayed with them for an open mind as they attended the meetings.

As one of the conference speakers, my emphasis was on forgiving people their trespasses whether they asked for it or not, or even if you never saw them again. Nursing a grudge within your own mind hurts no one else but you. You are a slave to the person you hate. Jesus said,

> "For if you forgive men their trespasses,
> your heavenly Father will also forgive you.
> But if you do not forgive men their trespasses,
> neither will your Father forgive your trespasses."
> MATTHEW 6:14–15

The other speaker taught from the Book of Galatians. The acts of the sinful nature block the fruit of the Spirit. The barrier is made out of sexual immorality, hatred, discord, fits of rage, jealousy, selfish ambition, dissensions, and envy.

To be filled with the Spirit means to be controlled by the Spirit. It is necessary to be filled with the Spirit in order to live the Christian life. "Why would anyone turn his back on an inner life like that?" the speaker asked.

Two days later the couple visited me. Clenched teeth and tight lips had become radiant smiles. They had just dropped in to let me know that they had listened and got their answers. They had dealt with their own sins. They did not need to talk to me anymore. Besides, they had to get to the lakeside to enjoy the afternoon.

Three months later, I received a phone call from them. All was well; he and his partner had resolved their differences.

It was a very complex problem, and I apparently had very little to do with the solution. This was God's doing, not mine. Was this too simple? We must be careful not to underestimate the help available to hungry, open-minded Christians from a prayer-filled conference.

God's Cleansing Power

Joe and Martha enjoyed the growing-up years of their son, Mike, his fun personality and bright mind. However, in high school he began withdrawing from the family. They passed it off as a phase in his life and dismissed it as peer pressure at school, but this only increased in his college years. At the age of twenty, after two years in college and while home for the summer, the problem came to a head.

About 1:00 A.M. they received a phone call. Mike said, "You'd better come down here." He had been speeding while drunk with three buddies in the car. He missed a right angle turn, drove off the end of the street into a driveway, rear-ended a parked car, shoved it through the corner of the garage, and wrecked his own car beyond repair. Mike was arrested, charged with drunk driving, and was being held at the police station. They would not release him, so his father returned home about 2:30 A.M.

They could no longer ignore the fact that they had been putting bandages on the problem for a long time. Martha and Joe slept no more that night. They began to face the reality that their son had emotionally departed some time ago. Bandages would not work; major changes were needed now. They finally concluded that they loved Mike so much and were willing to do whatever was necessary to help, including fighting for him.

Joe and Martha felt that Mike and his friends were not good for each other and the relationship should end. They realized that this might not be acceptable to him, and he might leave home as a result.

They decided to stop him if he tried to leave; and if he did leave, to go after him. For them to lose their son, he would have to reject their love. It would not be because they didn't love him enough to fight for him.

His father had to face another tough truth. He knew what he should do, but he had no confidence; his track record was not good, and his judgment was too subjective.

Realizing how important it was for them to make the right choices, they called me, an old friend who lived three thousand miles away in Florida.

We sat around the kitchen table while I asked questions and took notes. After about an hour and a half, I knew enough to say what they each needed to hear. "Joe, you have been foolish and need to repent. You said you knew Mike was not going in the right direction but, compared to yourself at his age, he wasn't doing too bad. Since when are you, at that age, God's standard for anybody? You also said you didn't want to drive Mike away. Mike, did you know that your dad didn't want to drive you away?"

Mike nodded.

"Martha, you have been foolish and need to repent. You have been trying to make your son happy. Stop playing God. Mike, did you know your mother wanted to make you happy?"

Mike nodded again.

Consider these verses for this family:

> **For whom the LORD loves He corrects,**
> **just as a father the son in whom he delights.**
> PROVERBS 3:12

> **Correct your son, and he will give you rest;**
> **yes, he will give delight to your soul.**
> PROVERBS 29:17

**The rod and rebuke give wisdom,
but a child left to himself brings shame to his mother.**
PROVERBS 29:15

Then I said, "Joe and Martha, you have a reasonably intelligent twenty-year-old son who has figured that his dad doesn't want to drive him away and that his mother wants to make him happy. He's been playing that for all it's worth.

"Your home has been a training center, but your son has been the trainer training his parents in the way he wants them to go. Allow what he wants, and he rewards you with a good attitude. Inhibit what he wants, and he penalizes you with a bad attitude. Your son has been controlling this home by his attitude."

I then turned to Mike. "Mike, you are an angry, deceitful young man. That's not my opinion but what you have revealed about yourself, and I recorded it in my notes. I don't need to meet your friends to know what they're like. They're just like you—that's why they are your friends.

"Mike, if you don't repent, I predict that this is your future: You will find some attractive young woman who is just like you. You'll seem to have a lot in common, think you're in love, marry, and then turn your anger and deceitfulness on each other and ruin each other's lives."

Looking at all three of them, I continued, "You each need to repent so that a real change takes place in your life." Martha and Joe needed to establish sensible limits for Mike and enforce them. Mike needed to repent of his rebellious, deceitful self-seeking and let God change him.

After that I could only say, "Well, I can't repent for you, so you might as well take me to the airport."

Martha and Joe repented, but Mike seemed cold and unresponsive until a couple of days later. He seemed so matter-of-fact, saying that he had repented and never really meant to hurt his parents. Although they had difficulty believing him, they perceived the counsel they had received had the ring of truth.

They decided that in the fall Mike should enroll in a school that would provide the helpful environment he needed to change. Of course, Mike did not want that kind of school environment; he wanted to continue living off campus, accountable to no one. At the same time, however, Mike didn't want to continue as before.

He resisted; and they persisted. Mike enrolled in a school with rules, lived on campus in a dorm with "nosy dorm leaders."

Their family struggled through a number of tear-filled incidents, but they didn't give up.

Imagine their surprise, when after getting his bachelor's degree in English, Mike decided to stay in the same school (with rules) and to pursue another degree in counseling. He chose another school (with rules) for his master's in counseling and then gained his doctorate at one of the leading universities in the nation. He is now married to a lovely Christian, and they are about to have their first child.

The core problem was with the parents even more so than with their son. He was more willing to receive correction and direction than they had been able or willing to provide it.

Does such a brief encounter as I had with this family have lasting results? This occurred ten years ago, and to date all is well with Mike.

Do not underestimate the cleansing power available when anyone approaches God as a repentant sinner who has seen his sin and wants to be restored and renewed. It doesn't take God long to transform a humble person.

A Listener with an Open Heart

Duke is the pastor of a church today. It was not always so. Duke was a very strong-willed child from the day he was born. At age seventeen he was in complete rebellion. He used drugs, stole, and was rude and obnoxious. His parents sought help from counselors, doctors, and the police, but none could help. He ran away from home for eleven weeks. Then he returned on his own. He continued his uncooperative, obnoxious ways. His father's job required travel, so his mother attempted to deal with their son. They restricted him to the house, but he refused to comply, threatening to leave again.

I was speaking on family relations when an elegantly dressed lady, looking as if she didn't have a care in the world, approached me after one session and asked if I could help her. She told me this story. She had run out of ideas and didn't know what else to do.

Knowing how to respond to such a problem with so little information is very difficult. At such a time I need to seek God, admit my helplessness, and appeal to Him for wisdom. Theoretically, I needed information: what is she like, what is her husband like, some history about Duke. Without proper information, how could I help?

My heart was filled with sympathy and compassion for this obviously desperate, anxious lady. It seemed logical to comfort her by reassuring her that it was quite normal to be anxious. However, that's not what I heard myself say. Instead, I told her that she had at least two problems, perhaps three.

First, she needed to relax.

Two Bible verses came to mind:

Trust in the LORD with all your heart,
and lean not on your own understanding;

**in all your ways acknowledge Him,
and He shall direct your paths.**

PROVERBS 3:5–6

**Let the peace of God rule in your hearts
. . . and be thankful.**

COLOSSIANS 3:15

Her response was total unbelief. How is it possible to calm down under these conditions and be thankful? I reminded her that, to say the least, she could be thankful that she had received a chance to be reminded that God would direct her path. She seemed more disturbed than ever.

Second, whatever she did about her son, she needed to be sure that she and her husband were like-minded about any action.

Third, I could not advise her specifically on what to do, but something, probably quite drastic, should be done quickly. I reminded her that she and her husband needed to trust the Lord and not be afraid of losing their son. They probably already had; this was the opportunity to win him back.

She left, looking more despondent than ever. A quick conversation immediately after a meeting is hard to handle. This one surely looked like a dud. My intentions were good, but it seemed that the more I tried to help, the more agitated she became. I have learned to depend upon a person's second reaction to a conversation rather than the first.

Several years later, a clean-cut young man came to the platform after a meeting and introduced himself.

"My name is Duke," he said, "I'm in college preparing for the ministry. I came to thank you for encouraging my parents not to give up on me."

Twenty years later, at another meeting, this same lady named Catherine and her husband Bob came up to me. I didn't recognize her. They gave me a report on Duke. He finished college and seminary, married a fellow student, and today they are pioneering the establishing of a new church.

Catherine told me what had happened after she left the meeting twenty years ago. She did have a second reaction. She had to admit that she had not considered it even remotely possible to relax. She was at her wits' end over what to do; professionals were no help. But she had not thought of turning the problem over to God and to consciously team up with her husband.

She and her husband renewed their commitment to do anything to save their son from sure destruction and to depend on God to direct their paths. Now Duke was up against two people renewed in their dedication to seek God's best for their son. They agreed to expect Duke to do what was right and to do whatever was necessary to enforce righteousness, whatever that meant.

These Scriptures would make a difference if applied to their lives:

Now I plead with you, brethren,
by the name of our Lord Jesus Christ,
that you all speak the same thing,
and that there be no divisions among you,
but that you be perfectly joined together
in the same mind and in the same judgment.

1 CORINTHIANS 1:10

He who spares his rod hates his son,
but he who loves him disciplines him promptly.

PROVERBS 13:24

A few days later, Duke and his father were in the kitchen, just the two of them. On the counter was a bottle of vitamins that his mother used. Duke wanted some of the vitamins. Bob was not sure if these were prescription drugs so he told Duke to ask his mother for permission. Duke cursed his mother, and Bob rebuked his son sharply. Duke swung at his dad; Bob knocked him to the floor. A vigorous fight followed. Duke managed to get away and took off on his bicycle. Bob went after him in his car but could not find him.

Bob returned home and went to Duke's room where he found a sizable quantity of marijuana. He went to the police station and swore out a warrant for his son's arrest.

Wow! Does this sound like the Lord directing Bob's path? This all took place on Mother's Day.

They accepted this crisis as God's leading. They were doing the best they knew how on behalf of their beloved son.

When Duke came home to pack up and leave, Catherine called the police. They arrived quickly, with not one but three cars with lights flashing, attracting the attention of the whole neighborhood. Two policemen arrested Duke, handcuffed him, and led him to a police car. Duke's sister and the neighbors were appalled.

The hearing was scheduled; bail was set high enough so that Duke's friends could not get him out for two weeks. Duke had bragged that the police would never catch him, but now he was in jail on a warrant sworn out by his own parents.

At the hearing Duke was sentenced to ten days in jail and one year of probation. While he was in jail, Duke refused to talk to his father. He would talk to his mother. She visited him and brought him reading material. While he served the ten days, a doctor discovered that Duke had a serious case of hypoglycemia.

When Duke began his probation, a police sergeant instructed him to fill out a daily report of his activities, accounting for each hour, and submit it weekly. He warned Duke that if he failed to submit the report, he would personally see to it that Duke would get a five-year sentence. He showed Duke pictures of several young men who called his bluff and who were all in prison. Duke was paroled into the custody of his parents.

Catherine nursed Duke back to health. He continued to ignore his father, but complied with the terms of his probation.

When Duke regained his health, he got a job with a contractor. It was a pick-and-shovel job, mostly with a partner. This fellow was annoyingly cheerful and considerate toward Duke. Day in and day out, week after week, this fellow lived a consistent, cheerful life. Every chance he got, he tried to tell Duke about Jesus, who saved him from a life of anger and misery.

One day Duke said, "Mom, guess what happened to me." Her heart sank. *What trouble is he in now?* she thought.

"I gave my heart to Jesus," he said, "From now on I'm living for God."

Duke then made a U-turn. He went to places where he had stolen things and made restitution. He changed his friends and graduated from college and seminary.

Today he is pastor of a church, and I had the pleasant surprise of having lunch with Duke recently. I asked him to tell me his memories of that period. Here are a few of his reflections:

> One day these two giant policemen walked into my room at home and arrested me. Man, they were prepared. They surrounded the house. They had a dog in case I tried to run away. Guns and everything. I sat in jail for two weeks before getting out.

But I didn't stop drugs. I just got smarter and more careful.

I had this job working for a construction company with a pick and shovel with this long-haired hippie that kept talking about Jesus. One day we were in the bottom of an empty swimming pool shoveling out slimy scum. Man, it was the worst job I have ever had—smelly, got all over you—yuck!

We took a short rest break, and the fellow with whom I was working told me about Jesus. Now a lot of things from that part of my life are a little confusing, having taken everything from LSD to you-name-it, but something clicked inside of me. What he said seemed to make sense. I went inside to wash my hands and face at lunchtime. When I looked up at the mirror to dry my face, I felt clean. I knew something had happened. I went out and told my working buddy that I had become a Christian.

Later, I told my drug friends about Jesus. They said, "Aw, you'll get over it. You're just going through a phase." Well, they may be right, but it's been over twenty years and I haven't gotten over it yet. You know, Dr. Brandt, there's another thing. I never quit doing drugs; I just didn't want them anymore.

Don't take too lightly the help that is available to a listener with an open heart. God had prepared a solution for that mother. Our brief encounter after a meeting had to be just a tiny part. My little advice motivated her to bring God in on the solution. It didn't seem very hopeful as she walked away from our little chat, but God's ways are not our ways.

Give Simplicity a Chance

Tim Daley is a biblical counselor. We have compared notes for years. Four hundred men were at a retreat to which he invited me. I was to learn that thirty-five of them were there because Tim's life had touched their lives.

Bert was one of the men at this conference. He had set up certain procedures for the insurance agents who worked for him to follow. One agent who refused to comply was Bert's older brother.

Over the next year the two of them had many strained and heated conversations about the issue. One day when they were angrily throwing verbal bricks at each other, his brother cleaned out his office and left. Bert called him on the phone a few days later. The verbal barrage continued until, finally, Bert hung up on his brother. He was livid with rage. There was no contact for a month.

Earlier, when his brother had come to work with Bert, they had agreed that any problem would be worked out amiably and that work details would not interfere with family ties. Yet here they were sharply divided and a major holiday was coming up.

Finally Bert consulted with Tim Daley, who listened intently to the story. Tim leaned forward and said, "You are a bitter, angry man. The way you talked to your brother is unacceptable as a Christian example. You need to repent and then apologize to your brother for your bad attitude. You will not find peace until you do."

End of interview.

Bert wasn't prepared for that. He was expecting some reassurance that he was justified in his response because of the problem his brother had created.

He pondered Tim's advice. He was afraid to call his brother, but the idea plagued him. Bert was reluctant to admit that he was bitter, angry, and self-righteous. Finally he admitted this to God with a repentant heart and asked to be cleansed and empowered to love his brother. To his surprise, his resistance to calling his brother turned into an urge to see him.

His brother didn't want to see him. Bert heard himself pleading for a twenty-minute meeting. It was agreed to reluctantly, and they met at the appointed place. His brother said nothing, but Bert felt compassion toward him. Gone was the bitterness. He proceeded to apologize for the attitude he had had toward his brother. He asked for forgiveness; his brother had tears in his eyes, as did Bert.

Bert said that at that moment it was as though a two-hundred-pound weight was lifted from his shoulders.

Years have passed. The problem is behind them. Allowing God to change his heart was the first step in changing a complex problem into a simple one. Bert was a repentant prayer away from a change of heart all the time.

There are many more such stories happening every day. Jesus said:

> **"Come to Me,**
> **all you who labor and are heavy laden,**
> **and I will give you rest."**
> MATTHEW 11:28

The psalmist said:

> **Cast your burden on the LORD,**
> **and He shall sustain you;**
> **He shall never permit**
> **the righteous to be moved.**
> PSALMS 55:22

"Moreover if your brother sins against you,
go and tell him his fault between you and him alone.
If he hears you,
you have gained your brother.
But if he will not hear you,
take with you one or two more,
that 'by the mouth of two or three witnesses
every word may be established.'
And if he refuses to hear them,
tell it to the church.
But if he refuses even to hear the church,
let him be to you like a heathen and a tax collector."

MATTHEW 18:15–17

"Brethren, if a man is overtaken in any trespass,
you who are spiritual
restore such a one in a spirit of gentleness,
considering yourself lest you also be tempted."

GALATIANS 6:1

I often have people tell me, "Dr. Brandt, it's just not that simple!" My reply is, "Have you tried it?"

Long pause. End of discussion. Many argue with me on this point—except my clients who have tried it.

CHAPTER 2

Peace and Satisfaction in This World?

Thought Starter

Why are Christians not in the least embarrassed over the absence of peace and rest in their lives?

◆

These things I have spoken to you,
that in Me you may have peace.
In the world you will have tribulation;
but be of good cheer,
I have overcome the world.

JOHN 16:33

Peace I leave with you,
My peace I give to you;
not as the world gives do I give to you.
Let not your heart be troubled,
neither let it be afraid.

JOHN 14:27

Jesus clearly tells us that it is His intention for us to move through this world peacefully and cheerfully, untroubled and unafraid; as long as we look to Him to enable us. With such a resource readily available, I am overwhelmed by the absence of personal peace and by the level of misery under which Christians are willing to live. Christians don't seem the least embarrassed or hesitant to declare:

- ◆ "I'm under stress."
- ◆ "I'm anxious."
- ◆ "I'm worried."
- ◆ "I'm angry!"
- ◆ "I'm so unhappy."
- ◆ "I can't get along with him [her]."
- ◆ "I'm afraid."

Christians all too frequently and unabashedly accept the word of secular mental health people who tell us that such conditions are socially and culturally caused and relief is to be found in the world. In one sense they are correct. Jesus Himself said you can find peace in the world.

Jesus tells us that He can cause us to move through this troubled world peacefully, cheerfully, untroubled, and unafraid:

> **These things I have spoken to you,**
> **that in Me you may have peace.**
> **In the world you will have tribulation;**
> **but be of good cheer,**
> **I have overcome the world.**
> JOHN 16:33

What will you do with Jesus and His words in this verse? He says you can have peace in this world by turning either to Him or to the world (your environment) that He created. I see many Christians adopt, without thinking, a so-what-never-mind-what-Jesus-said attitude and turn to the world in search of peace. Let's take a look at what the world offers:

- ◆ Places
- ◆ Activities and events
- ◆ Things
- ◆ People

Peace and Places

I stepped out of the car at the Horn Creek Conference Center in the mountains near Colorado Springs and took a deep breath of clean mountain air. The spectacular Rocky Mountains rimmed the valley where I stood.

We all know that feeling of traveling a long way and experiencing the anticipation and then the excitement of arrival; that's what I felt. Hiking in the mountains, walking beautiful trails, fishing in a stream, or just standing by a gorgeous waterfall are each a source of anticipated relaxation.

Recently I visited my son-in-law in Idaho. I sat in the living room and looked out over a golden grain field that extended out from the backyard. In the distance I could see the foothills rising to meet the clear Idaho sky. From the front porch you could see a pasture with sheep grazing. What a peaceful place this is!

Interacting alone with this magnificent creation can quiet one's heart. Unfortunately, conflict with one another, even in the most scenic places, will steal away that peace.

A couple was experiencing serious marital problems. The husband surprised his wife with a first-class deluxe Caribbean cruise. The drive to the boat dock was pleasant as they anticipated all the fun they would have on the ship for a week in the sun.

When they entered their small, narrow stateroom, the husband quickly changed into his loudest multicolored shirt (which his wife intensely disliked), threw the first shirt on the floor in the corner (she liked to keep a neat house), and pressured his wife with, "Honey, will you please hustle it up!" (He liked to be on time, and she was always late.) On the deck, he, being an extrovert, began to loudly introduce himself to people. She, being an introvert, was embarrassed by his loudness and his awful shirt. They both wanted to accomplish something in their relationship that they couldn't do at home. Needless to say, the Caribbean cruise was a disaster because they brought themselves along.

Sadly, we all know that peace inside an individual is not determined by being in a place.

Peace and Activities

You can feel fulfilled by being involved in study programs in a wide variety of schools, colleges, institutes, and universities.

You can feel challenged by the pursuit of a career or hobbies, learning a skill, becoming involved in a cause, attending an event, helping with charitable work, becoming involved in an exercise or weight-loss program or even working long and diligent hours in Christian work. Many activities can give satisfaction and pleasure to the participants without their giving God a thought.

I met a prominent lawyer who was to introduce me as a banquet speaker. I asked him how he became a Christian.

He told me he had been a star athlete and the top student in high school. When he received his diploma, he was disappointed. He had thought there would be more satisfaction than he experienced. He entered Harvard College and received recognition and satisfaction from playing on the varsity football team. In the classroom he was a top student. But when he received his diploma, he was disappointed not to experience satisfaction from this accomplishment. So he looked eagerly to law school at Yale, completing that program with top honors.

Once again, receiving his diploma left him with a vague feeling of emptiness and the thought that there must be more to life than this. When he received an invitation to join the prestigious law firm of his choice, his career was off to a good start. Then he and his wife designed and built their dream house. They looked forward to the day they would take possession; when that day came, there was no joy. There was an emptiness that career and marriage could not fill. "When that day came," he said, "we realized there had to be more to life than this!"

He looked straight at me. "At that time I met a businessman with a serenity about him that caught my attention. In a conversation over lunch one day, I asked him why he seemed so content with life. He is the one who introduced me to the resources that are available to us from God. And that's why I am here to introduce you, Dr. Brandt."

The attorney found the flaw in depending on activities and events: they eventually come to an end and leave you empty.

This is me - Busy but not fulfilled -

Peace and Things

This amazing world is filled with interesting things that can satisfy a restless heart and bring peace and contentment. We are all familiar with the calming effect of a pleasurable drive in a car. House furnishings, TVs, VCRs and stereos are pleasurable adult toys.

Most of us can recall happy moments enjoying a delicious meal together. Buying clothes and looking after the hair, the face, and the body are pleasant activities. The lawn, flowers, bushes, trees, and shrubs can provide hours of enjoyment and relaxation. Alcohol is the oil that eliminates social friction. Swallowing pills can calm you down or pick you up.

I was working with a gentleman who was a highly successful and prominent engineer. He invited me to his home. His driveway was a quarter of a mile long; as we approached the house, I saw the six-car garage with a car in each one. The home had a butler, a chauffeur, a gardener, two maids, a nanny, and a cook. The acreage was large and very private, with a horse stable, a swimming pool, and a tennis court. We had our own private accommodations in a separate wing of the house. He had everything money could buy, but his family was in shambles.

At a family life conference at which I had spoken during the previous year, he realized his life was empty and that during the accumulation of all his wealth, he had neglected his wife and family. At the conference he had committed to establish a positive relationship with his family.

My purpose during this visit, a year after his first con-ference, was to see if I could help overcome some of the bar-riers that separated him from his wife and family. Sadly, as it turned out, his wife was not even willing to consider a closer relationship with him at this time. Here was the display of all the things money could buy. It was also a stark reminder that there are some things money cannot buy: the spirit of love, joy, peace, and kindness flowing back and forth between par-ents, partners, and children. Today he remains committed to his goal with his family, but it may take a long time.

Peace and People

"Greater love has no one than this,
than to lay down one's life for his friends.
You are My friends if you do whatever I command you."
JOHN 15:13–14

An obvious pathway to find relief from tension and stress is to pour out our thoughts and feelings to a sympathetic lis-tener. I've spent most of my life as a counselor, and I can assure you that you can find relief through counseling and therapy without giving God a thought.

A newspaper report on a conference of survivors of suicides featured one mother's story. Her world ended on the day her son killed himself. She told other survivors of suicides that their feelings of anguish, anger, and guilt are normal. Eventually she allowed her feelings of guilt to wash away when her therapist helped her realize she wasn't to blame.[1]

One human being helping another: a pat on the back, a friendly hug, or a compliment from someone you care about is delightfully soothing.

The sympathy and affection that self-help groups give each other is often the only source of help that keeps many a weary soul from giving up. Every Monday, a list of dozens of support groups appears in our local paper. Table 1 lists some of the groups:

Table 1: Support Groups	
Mended Hearts, Inc.	Smokers Anonymous
Alcoholics Anonymous	Food Addicts Anonymous
Bereavement Support Group	People Who Love Too Much
Compassionate Friends	Narcotics Anonymous
Emotions Anonymous	Family, Friends, and Lovers (AIDS)
Women Who Love Too Much	Take Off Pounds Sensibly
Arthritis Foundation	Co-dependents in Relationships
Living with Breast Cancer	Adult Children of Alcoholics
Caregivers Support Group	Rebuilders (divorced&separated)
Overeaters Anonymous	Children with Learning Disabilities
Coping with Cancer	Alliance for the Mentally Ill
Miscarriage Support Group	Hospice Bereavement Support Group
Alzheimer's Support Group	Impaired Nurses Support Group
M.A.D.D.	Support Group for Interfaith Couples
Nursing Home Support Group	C.A.R.P. Parent Support Group (Families affected by drug and alcohol abuse)

A pleasing sense of belonging and approval comes as a part of a cooperative effort, such as playing on a team, sharing a work project, sensing the appreciative response of others in the use of your talents.

And what can be more satisfying than for a young man and a young lady to meet and experience an irresistible attraction toward one another that deepens into a satisfying relationship? Finally these two, usually opposites, gradually blend their lives into a partnership.

There is just something special and satisfying about a deepening friendship between two people, male or female, which contains the unmistakable comfort of heart-to-heart talks. Teaching, learning, and serving also give a sense of accomplishment that is deeply satisfying. Why then doesn't it work?

Peace and Jesus

I have attempted to create a picture of the finest and best features in this wonderful world. The humanist is right: This world contains ample resources that, coupled with the best efforts of caring people, *should* result in a world full of satisfied, happy people. But, alas, there is a flaw in this beautiful picture.

You would think you could find continuous satisfaction, peace, and enjoyment from family life, social life, friendships, school and church associates, and professional contacts without giving God a thought.

As I reflect across the last decade, the death of my late wife Eva interrupted that human fellowship. I married again and three years later my wife Marcey died suddenly. Jim Baker, one of my best friends who traveled with me all over the world, suddenly died of a brain aneurysm; he was only fifty-two. Art DeMoss, a fifty-three-year-old businessman with whom I have shared ministry assignments many times, died of a heart attack on the tennis court. A college official whom I respected greatly suddenly announced that he was resigning his position, divorcing his wife, and marrying someone else. Just weeks ago, a tearful young lady with two young children told me that her husband had announced that he was leaving her. No warning. No explanation.

Time, on September 15, 1986, reported that the health cost of drug abuse was estimated by one National Center for Health statistics study at $59.7 billion. The medical bill for alcohol abuse was estimated at an astonishing $146.7 billion.

Earlier in this chapter, I wrote optimistically about the pleasures of courtship that deepens into a happy, lifetime marriage. Present reality shatters that beautiful hope when we read the latest statistics on divorce.

I wrote of the benefits of friendship, cooperation, teamwork, and recognition. To my dismay, I listen to a daily recital of the failure of human effort, of marriage partners who have deceived and cheated each other. We have become accustomed to reports of lying, cheating, and stealing in business and politics. There is strife and discord at every level of life: from the boardroom to the classroom to the family room.

The Florida legislature is currently struggling with what to do to halt teenage pregnancy. In 1991 about twenty-five thousand teenagers gave birth last year in Florida, costing more than $125 million in subsidized health care and welfare payments. More than one million teenagers became pregnant in the same year in our country, and almost half chose to have abortions. Ninety-two percent of these pregnancies were unintended.

In this wonderful world, families are breaking up; incidents of child abuse and other family violence are growing; and delinquency, theft, murder, crime, escalating venereal diseases, and emotional disorders threaten our survival. There are multitudes starving to death, and nations are destroying each other.

We must find relief from tension. People often turn to friendship, fellowship, challenges, opportunities, travel, and materialism, but they are as illusive as turning to drugs and alcohol. Initially there is hope, comfort, pleasure; but sooner or later our efforts turn to ashes and result in increased loneliness, grief, tension, or bitterness.

The Humanist Manifesto II says: "Happiness and the creative realization of human needs and desires, individually and in shared enjoyment, are continuous themes of humanism. Critical intelligence, infused by a sense of human caring, is the best method that humanity has for resolving problems" (p.18).

It seems clear to me that the finest human effort in a magnificent world is not enough to quiet the human heart in times of trouble and stress.

Jesus said:

> "These things I have spoken to you,
> that in Me you may have peace.
> In the world you will have tribulation;
> but be of good cheer,
> I have overcome the world."
>
> JOHN 16:33

Based on all the options we have for going after peace, we should take careful note when Jesus gently tells us to turn to Him for peace. We can turn to Him and not the world, if the peace we seek is to be deeply satisfying and lasting.

CHAPTER 3

Most of Us Had a Poor Start in Life!

Thought Starter

Why do people blame their present behavior
on their past experiences?

◆

Beware lest anyone cheat you
through philosophy and empty deceit,
according to the tradition of men,
according to the basic principles of the world,
and not according to Christ.
For in Him dwells all the fullness of the Godhead bodily;
and you are complete in Him,
who is the head of all principality and power.
COLOSSIANS 2:8–10

Malcolm and Dorothy sit, stone-faced, across from the counselor in the consulting room with an invisible wall between them. They are very busy Christians who have been married for twenty-two miserable years.

She says that he does not treat her like a doormat but like the dirt under a doormat! She would do anything in the world for him, she says: "If only he would show some appreciation and give me just a little bit of affection and tenderness. But no, he just takes me for granted. All he wants is for me to wash his clothes, cook his meals, and keep the house. He is a very proud, selfish, bad-tempered man given to very loud yelling."

To show how inconsiderate he is, she tells how he bought her the Lincoln she drives when he knew perfectly well that she wanted a Cadillac. She must even beg him for a meager allowance. The counselor, however, looks at a well-groomed, elegantly dressed lady and observes that underneath the expensive clothing is a very hostile, bitter woman.

They live in a large, professionally decorated, color-coordinated, beautifully furnished and landscaped house. They could not wish for a better, more air-conditioned place in which to carry on their bitter relationship. Their two children live on the opposite side of the country and as far away from their parents as they could get. The maid does her best to avoid getting chewed out by either one of them.

Malcolm sits there shaking his head, teeth clenched, as he listens to her side of the story. When it is his turn he describes her as a spoiled, selfish, demanding person. From the start of their marriage everything had to go her way, from keeping the house, to when they ate, choosing friends and activities, raising the children, choosing their clothes, and on and on. He finally gave up on her and concentrated on developing his business. He let her run the house and the family. He had his territory; she had hers. Their buffer zone was the children. Now the children are gone and all that is left between them is mutual hostility and strong differences of opinion.

Malcolm had been raised in a lower class European family where the father called all the shots and the women followed instructions. His father had a violent temper and would abuse the family verbally and sometimes physically. Malcolm is much like his father, except he never physically abused anyone. He admits to being self-centered.

Dorothy grew up in an upper middle-class home. She had very few limits, was quite self-centered, and often pouted when she couldn't have her way. She could be called a spoiled child. Her parents provided a stable home and her mother tended to dominate the family.

Obviously there is more to each of their histories. But at this point she will only admit to being a misunderstood lady and this brings great frustration to her.

When this couple began to seek help, they could have turned to a counselor with either a humanist or a biblical perspective. The two approaches would be quite different.

The study of how humans affect or help one another is humanism.

Webster's dictionary defines *humanism* as, "A doctrine, set of attitudes, a way of life centered upon human interests or values; a philosophy that rejects supernaturalism, regards man as a natural object, and asserts the essential dignity and worth of man and his capacity to achieve self-realization through the use of reason and scientific method."

Although the name is current, humanism, as a philosophy of life, is nothing new. Rejecting God and centering a way of life and a way of thinking around man's interests and values has been around since the beginning of time.

Don't Blame Your Background

In graduate school my professors identified a rather predictable response caused by growing up in a restrictive environment. They identified a poor start in life as one that hinders self-expression, frustrates pleasure needs, and provides wrong reinforcers.

They taught that the consequences of growing up in this type of environment are adults who will respond to the circumstances of life with the following ways:

Responses That Humanists Believe Are Caused by Our Environment		
Hostility	Resentment	Hate
Pessimism	Fear	Doubt
Perplexity	Conflict	Confusion
Pain	Depression	Indifference
Cruelty	Lack of generosity	Rage
Oppression of others		

Time magazine featured an article entitled "The Burnout of Almost Everyone:" "They describe the stages of burnout, progressing from intense enthusiasm and job satisfaction, to exhaustion, physical illness, acute anger and depression. Even the best worker, when thwarted, will swallow his rage; it then turns into a small private conflagration, an internal fire in his engine room."[1]

According to these authors, the consequences to adults of being thwarted (i.e., not getting their own way) by other adults (i.e., husbands and wives) are rage and hostility, resulting in physical illness, depression, and tension headaches.

No doubt people who struggle with the responses listed above do come from faulty family backgrounds, unloving relationships, difficult experiences, and situations in which there was little opportunity given to express themselves.

Furthermore, given proper alteration in the people, circumstances, and social conditions that surround an individual, changes can occur without giving God a thought. Counseling, done by trained, caring, kind people, followed by appropriate changes, can bring great relief to an anxious, confused person. If you want relief, you can find it in this wonderful world. Many ask, "Who needs God?"

A change of location or the removal of a troublesome person can give relief to an anxious person. That is relief, not healing. Alcohol can quiet a hostile, bitter heart, but it only gives relief, not healing.

If the couple we described at the beginning of this chapter would turn to a humanist counselor for help, the counselor would develop a detailed study of their backgrounds, their stormy marriage, and their response to each other at present. From this information, the counselor would help them understand how their backgrounds have shaped their outlook on life, what their needs are, what ways they are frustrating each other's needs, and what adjustments can be made in order to satisfy each other's needs.

Understand Relief Versus Healing

Hopefully, as Dorothy gains some understanding of both her needs and Malcolm's, and senses that he is making adjustments with her needs in mind, her anger and bitterness will be calmed and she will experience some peace of mind, become more hopeful, more affectionate, and more desirous of meeting his needs.

As Malcolm gains some understanding of his and Dorothy's needs, makes some adjustments on her behalf, and senses that she is seeking to meet his needs, his quarrelsomeness and hot temper will cool. They can then develop a friendship and discover the joy of living as he works to meet her needs.

Just imagine how relieved these people would be if the counselor could help them in this way.

I emphasize that they can find blessed relief by following this approach, but not a change of heart.

What causes change as a result of relief? We could compare this change to the relief experienced if you take a pain pill. Change happens swiftly. You get relief but not healing. Isn't it good to get relief? Of course, as long as you don't kid yourself, and you understand it is relief and not healing.

Recently, I learned a lesson about the quick, comforting effect of drugs. I had a tooth pulled and developed what my dentist called a "dry socket." My jaw became infected and it spread to the side of my face so that at any one moment I experienced incredible, unbearable pain around my eye, ear, sinuses, jaw, and throat. The pain was so intense I was ready to do anything for some relief!

My dentist handed me an envelope containing some little pills. After swallowing one, the pain gradually disappeared. To maintain freedom from pain, all I had to do was keep swallowing those pills.

Everyone knows that pain pills do not cure the source of the pain. Healing must also happen. So I knew that the condition of my jaw had not changed. But that didn't matter. I would have paid *any* price for those pills. (This incident was a clear lesson to me of how easily anyone can become dependent on pills for a sense of well-being.) Having one's needs met, similarly, brings relief, not healing.

Our couple could seek out a Christian who is trained in humanistic counseling, who would proceed in the same methods as the humanistic counselor. They could seek out a biblical counselor, who would also recognize that the woman's anger, her bitter response to her husband, and his quarrelsomeness and nasty temper were barriers to a healthy marriage. The humanist would say these responses are socially caused. The Bible-based counselor would call them sin.

A very, very, very important decision: By faith the humanist says that anger, bitterness, quarrelsomeness, or a nasty temper is caused by the way you have been treated. By faith, the biblical counselor says that these characteristics are caused by sin. By faith, what do you say? Your decision will determine where you turn for help!

If you fail to deal with the sin, the relief you experience is like taking a pain pill for a toothache without fixing the tooth.

What is the sin that I Did? I want to know! Help Lord!

Blame Your Sin

Finding relief from sin instead of obtaining cleansing is a cruel trap. Like my situation with the pain pill, I am comfortably sick. Relief from sin allows me to be comfortably separated from God.

A follower of Jesus takes the subject of sin seriously. We do indeed face very serious social problems. If it is sin that is the cause, there couldn't be any better news: *There is a cure for sin.*

Many years ago, I contracted malaria. I alternately perspired and shivered, my joints ached, and I struggled with a high fever. One of the missionaries said, "It's only malaria. Take these pills and go to bed. Tomorrow you will be better." Sure enough, it worked.

Several years later my wife and her friend who traveled with us in a part of Africa became very ill after we returned home to the United States. They had the same malaria symptoms that I had had previously, and they tried to tell their doctor what it was. He wouldn't listen, hospitalized them, and subjected them to a variety of tests and x-rays. In the meantime they both suffered with high fever, chills, and pain. Three days later the doctor consulted a tropical medicine specialist who diagnosed malaria. He prescribed the same pills I had taken and in one day they were better. They went through five days of unnecessary suffering because the doctor didn't know what to treat.

Dealing with sin is like that. The cure is swift and sure if you use the proper diagnosis and proper treatment. You can suffer greatly from the ravages of sin while you are sincerely and carefully trying to correct the suffering by following the wrong diagnosis and the wrong treatment.

In the case of my wife and her friend, the doctor had never seen malaria and therefore tried to find a cause familiar to him.

The same can happen when one deals with symptoms the Bible calls sin. There is no debate about the symptoms; everyone agrees on what they are. What is debatable is the cause.

The Bible says contention and outbursts of anger are works of the flesh or sin. If one or both people in a disagreement accept this diagnosis, they will turn God-ward, confess their sins, repent, and receive forgiveness, cleansing, and renewal.

If they reject the diagnosis as sin and believe the very same symptoms are socially or culturally caused, they will proceed to investigate exposure to family, friends, church, community, and so forth, for an explanation.

Dr. S. I. McMillen, a long-time friend of mine, spent many years studying the biblical principles and directions for living in Jewish and Christian writings. As a result of this research he wrote a best seller called *None of These Diseases*, which describes the physical consequences of wrong living. He pointed out that there may be sin in the picture when aches and pains show up:

Peace does not come in capsules! This is regrettable because medical science recognizes that emotions such as fear, sorrow, envy, resentment, and hatred are responsible for the majority of our sicknesses. Estimates vary from 60 percent to nearly 100 percent. Emotional stress can cause high blood pressure, toxic goiter, migraine headaches, arthritis, apoplexy, heart trouble, gastrointestinal ulcers, and other serious diseases too numerous to mention. As physicians we can prescribe medicine for the symptoms of these diseases, but we cannot do much for the underlying cause, emotional turmoil. It is lamentable that peace does not come in capsules. We need something more than a pill for the disease-producing stresses of the man who has lost his life's savings, the tearful feminine soul who has been jilted, the young father who has an inoperable cancer, the woman whose husband is a philanderer, the distraught teenager with a facial birthmark, and the schemer who lies awake at night trying to think of ways to get even with his neighbor . . . No one can appreciate so fully as a doctor the amazingly large percentage of human disease and suffering which is directly traceable to worry, fear, conflict, immorality, dissipation, and ignorance, to unwholesome thinking and unclean living. The sincere acceptance of the principles and teachings of Christ with respect to the life of mental peace and joy, the life of unselfish thought and clean living, would at once wipe out more than half the difficulties, diseases, and sorrows of the human race.[2]

A Christian with a biblical perspective and a Christian with a humanistic perspective can both be sincere, committed people who are looking at the same situation, but they will come up with different causes and different solutions.

Alexander Pope described how sin captures us:

> *Vice is a monster of so frightful mien,*
> *As to be hated needs but to be seen;*
> *Yet seen too oft, familiar with her face,*
> *We first endure, then pity, then embrace.*

Humanistic thinking can be like that. First, we study it in order to understand it. Then we shake our heads in disagreement, then listen some more to be sure we heard correctly, and finally, unknowingly, begin to absorb it.

If you are dealing with sin, you must turn to the Creator and Savior for cleansing, strengthening, and changing. If it is sin, society didn't put it into you; society only stirs up what is already in you. If it is sin, society can't help you. It requires a supernatural cure.

If you want relief, you can find it in this world. If you want a cure, only God can help you.

The Miracle of a Cleansed Life

The couple in this lesson became my clients. They had been to three counselors before coming to see me. One counselor was a humanist and not a Christian, and the other two were "Christian humanists." The counselors had actually worked with the couple individually and had gone into a detailed study of both their backgrounds, reviewing their twenty-year history of antagonism and discord. The couple came away from the counselors with the verdict that they had irreconcilable differences and divorce was the only solution.

But during the time with each previous counselor, the woman had come away from each session greatly relieved. She was appreciative of their understanding, kindness, and willingness to listen to her. She felt they understood that she was ready to change but her husband wouldn't cooperate. She felt the counselors understood why she was bitter and hostile under the circumstances with which she had to live.

The husband was very disgusted with the whole process. He tolerated going only for the sake of the marriage. In his opinion, they just sided with her and did not really grasp what a problem she had created for him in their marriage. So, as a result, she was helped in finding great relief for herself, but the marriage was actually worse.

It was immediately evident to me that she had two problems: first, a personal problem of sin in the areas of anger and bitterness, and second, the marriage.

He had two problems also: first, the personal problem of sin in the areas of quarrelsomeness and a nasty temper, and second, the marriage.

They turned to God for their solution and in six weeks they were behaving like honeymooners! Interestingly, I never did talk to them about their marriage.

I am not trying to say that their marriage problems evaporated. What I am saying is that they now approached their problems without hostility, quarreling, and yelling as they allowed the Lord to give them peaceful, loving, and joyful hearts. At that point they didn't need me and were quite capable of approaching their marriage problems in a friendly fashion and beginning to solve them.

This is the Christian miracle of the cleansed life—a great mystery—why, after years of fighting, would Malcolm and Dorothy submit to these biblical guidelines?

> But now you must also put off all these:
> anger, wrath, malice, blasphemy,
> filthy language out of your mouth.
> COLOSSIANS 3:8

> Therefore, as the elect of God, holy and beloved,
> put on tender mercies, kindness, humbleness,
> meekness, long-suffering.
> COLOSSIANS 3:12

Examine yourself. Are you a Christian who turns to God for help? Are you a Christian and a partial humanist who turns to the environment for relief from sin? Are you a humanist who accepts scientific investigation only and rejects the biblical record?

Here is His promise:

> For I know the thoughts that I think toward you,
> says the LORD,
> thoughts of peace and not of evil,
> to give you a future and a hope.
> Then you will call upon Me and go and pray to Me,
> and I will listen to you.
> And you will seek Me and find Me,
> when you search for Me with all your heart.
> JEREMIAH 29:11–13

CHAPTER 4

God's Sharpest Tools; My Biggest Problems

Thought Starter

Can you explain the change in some people's lives
when they became Christians?

♦

**Now if I do what I will not to do,
it is no longer I who do it,
but sin that dwells in me.**
ROMANS 7:20

**That which is born of the flesh is flesh,
and that which is born of the Spirit is spirit.
Do not marvel that I said to you,
You must be born again.**
JOHN 3:6–7

Born Again

I have spent over fifty years counseling people from a biblical perspective. I work with disturbed people. My first serious encounter with a disturbed person was with myself.

I grew up in a church environment. During my late teens, I said to myself, "I don't need a bunch of rules to run my life, let alone a bunch of rules that keep me from having fun!"

I had some friends who taught me how much fun I could have with alcohol. I hit the bars, the parties, the streets, and the homes of my friends (when the parents were gone!). Mixed in with all this was considerable girl-chasing. My mission in life was to entice "religious" young people away from church and into the "good life." I had been successful with my share of converts at the bar. Those were wonderful, fun-filled years, but such a life was also the broad road to destruction.

My way of life came to an abrupt halt. Three of my drinking buddies burned to death in a fiery head-on collision. One of my friends, a brilliant young lady, committed suicide. The heavy-drinking, kindly man who ran the pool room, one of my local hang-outs, slammed his car into a telephone pole one night and was killed instantly. Then I was fired from my job because I returned from lunch drunk one day.

Right after all this happened, Bill, one of my best friends and the heaviest drinker of all, suddenly announced that he had become a Christian. He had wandered into a Christian meeting by accident and stayed to hear the speaker. God's Holy Spirit touched his heart. He went forward at the end of the meeting and publicly invited Christ to take over his life and heart and to deal with his sin.

Virtually overnight Bill demonstrated that he was finished with my kind of life. He went to church twice on Sunday and every Wednesday. He dated only "Christian" girls. He limited his activities to swimming, hiking, tennis, ice-skating, and skiing. In order to continue my friendship with him, I was forced to accept his way of life.

For a few months I lived on both sides of the fence. Bill and I had long arguments about his faith and his changed life. I argued fervently on behalf of the old way of life, the rollicking nights, the warmth of kindred spirits and good fellowship in our favorite bars! I could just as well have been talking to the wall. Bill's change wasn't temporary. He turned a deaf ear to my fervent, earnest efforts to save him from a restrictive, limited, narrow life.

Encounter with the Stove Man

One afternoon I staggered home drunk and dropped off to sleep on the couch. A Christian businessman who had come to sell my mother a stove shook me awake. He read me a simple tract about receiving Christ. I had heard this familiar old story all my life. He asked me to pray with him, and in a drunken stupor, I asked the Lord to come into my heart. I then rolled over and went back to sleep!

Later in the evening, when I awoke, my only thought was to return to my favorite bar. That night the people around the bar seemed to be babbling, slurring their words, and talking foolishly. The bartender was carelessly sloshing the glasses in dirty water. The room was smoke-filled and unbearably noisy. I didn't have fun that night.

I found myself at the beginning of the end of my drinking days. In a matter of weeks, I longed for Bill's way of life. The old way simply died away. I didn't even remember the encounter with the stove salesman until I began looking back later on my changed behavior.

What followed in my life proved to me with abundant clarity that God will answer a sincere call for help even if the prayer is mumbled by someone who drinks too much, who slurs his words, and whose memory is blurred. Looking back on that event years ago, all I can remember of the discussion with the man in our living room is that what he said seemed to make sense.

I have a Ph.D. in marriage and the family and have spent my life studying, teaching, and counseling in the area of Christian living. Today, fifty years later, I still cannot totally explain what happened to me when I was "born again", or even why it happened to me. When Nicodemus, one of the smartest and most educated men of his day, asked Jesus, "What in the world are you talking about when you say, 'born again'?", Jesus replied:

> "Most assuredly,
> I say to you,
> unless one is born of water and the Spirit,
> he cannot enter the kingdom of God.
> That which is born of the flesh is flesh,
> and that which is born of the Spirit is spirit.
> Do not marvel that I said to you,
> 'You must be born again.'

> The wind blows where it wishes,
> and you hear the sound of it,
> but cannot tell where it comes from and where it goes.
> So is everyone who is born of the Spirit."

JOHN 3:5–8

Sin's Grasp

Swearing, drinking, and antagonism toward the church dropped away like dead leaves, but over a period of several years my sense of closeness to the Lord began to fade. Marriage, parenthood, and work revealed deeper life problems of anger, bitterness, hostility, and pride.

My boss was a harsh, cussing man. Day after day he would scowl as he scanned the engineering department from his glass-walled office. Stuffing his mouth with a huge chunk of tobacco, he would yell, "Brandt!" And that was all it took! Anger would well up within me and I was a goner! It worked every time; I was helpless. Even before his merciless tongue-lashings, I would be brimming with hostility and wounded pride.

How could I vent my feelings toward him? I would have found myself out in the street! As a result of keeping my anger inside, it spilled over into my relationships with my wife, my son, and my associates. I was filled with regret over the things I said and did. Telling myself to stop didn't help. I tried everything I could to find relief: taking a walk, griping to a friend, playing tennis, yelling at my wife or tiny son. *I even consciously thought about swearing and drinking again!* Typical regressive behavior. I even tried looking into my neglected Bible.

I quickly found out that Bible-reading was not easy. I couldn't scan the Bible and ignore parts of it like reading a newspaper. What I read was disturbing, but some of it slipped into my mind and I found myself comparing my behavior to the verses that I read.

I came upon a verse that got my attention:

> **Let all bitterness, wrath, anger, clamor,**
> **and evil speaking be put away from you,**
> **with all malice.**
> **And be kind to one another,**
> **tenderhearted, forgiving one another,**
> **just as God in Christ forgave you.**
> EPHESIANS 4:31–32

I spent several months contemplating those verses. They made me mad! The more I thought about forgiving my boss, my family and my associates, the more reasons I found for *not* forgiving them. I easily justified my hatred and anger. Why should I be kind and tenderhearted toward them? Such an idea infuriated me!

Eventually I came to the conclusion that the Bible was right. I told myself, "I will quit being hateful and angry toward these people." But as the days passed, I made a scary and frustrating discovery: I couldn't quit! When my boss yelled at me or my wife didn't do what I asked her to do, my response was automatic: intense anger! I could cover it up, put a smile on my face, and control my speech, but just underneath the surface was a furious response.

My resentment toward the Bible intensified. Here was a book that required something that I didn't want to do and couldn't do *even after I decided to do it!*

I identified with the Apostle Paul when he described himself:

> For the good that I will *to do,*
> I do not do;
> but the evil I will not *to do,*
> that I practice.
> Now if I do what I will not *to do,*
> it is no longer I who do it,
> but sin that dwells in me.
>
> ROMANS 7:19–20

As I continued to thumb through my Bible, I stumbled upon some verses which hit me right between the eyes:

> Not that we are in any way
> confident of doing anything by our own resources:
> our ability comes from God.
> It is He who makes us
> competent administrators of the new agreement,
> concerned not with the letter but with the Spirit.
> The letter of the law leads to the death of the soul;
> the Spirit alone can give life.
>
> 2 CORINTHIANS 3:5–6, PHILLIPS

Your Resources Are Not Enough

My response to those verses was troubled. Why couldn't I depend upon my own resources for living? *I* earned an education without God's help. *I* obtained a job and promotions. By my own will *I* managed to meet the demands of life. It appeared to me that *I* could do some things on *my own!*

After a long struggle I realized that what *I could not do* is live up to the *spirit* of Christianity. I could live up to "the letter" by acting kind, tenderhearted, and forgiving. But I found that *acting* killed something in me; it was death to my soul. The Christian life was not the development of my acting ability! The Christian life was God's Spirit living His life in me.

After admitting that my own resources were not enough, I faced other spiritual obstacles: Why did my fellowship with Jesus fade after my conversion? Why did God seem so distant, so unconcerned? Worst of all, why did God sometimes seem not to exist at all?

The Bible met all my questions with a single answer:

> **Behold, the LORD's hand is not shortened,**
> **that it cannot save;**
> **nor His ear heavy,**
> **that it cannot hear.**
> **But your iniquities have separated you from your God;**
> **and your sins have hidden His face from you,**
> **so that He will not hear.**
>
> ISAIAH 59:1–2

The Bible pointed out the problem: sin was keeping me at a distance from the Lord. Those verses that disturbed me said it all:

> **Let all bitterness, wrath, anger, clamor,**
> **and evil speaking be put away from you,**
> **with all malice.**
>
> EPHESIANS 4:31

These were the sins that made God seem so distant to me. My boss and family didn't cause them; they were only used to reveal them in me.

Since only God could cleanse me from sin, I asked Him to cleanse my heart. I also asked the Lord for help because I knew I couldn't help myself. I couldn't love my boss or my wife or my little boy. Oh, yes, I could *seem* loving, but that's not the same as *being* loving on the inside. The turning point came when I admitted to God that I was helpless and asked Him to give me His love for my boss when he was yelling at me. The next day on the way to work I again appealed to God to take away the intense anger when my boss yelled at me and give me His love for my boss.

I remember very well the day when my boss, his jaw loaded with tobacco, shouted, "Brandt!" and to my surprise, I wasn't mad at him. For the first time that I could remember, the smile on my face reflected my spirit. What an incredible experience for me! I'm not trying to say that I entrusted every day to the Lord. But every day that I did, I found the Lord was always there.

A few weeks later, my boss yelled at me again: "Brandt! Come in here!" By now he amused me. I actually enjoyed watching him! What a different experience it was when there was joy in my heart! I could watch an old crab and not become a crab myself! It was wonderful to be released from that trap. I walked into his office feeling friendly and relaxed. I asked, "What do you want?" And he said, "What's gotten into you? You've been in a good mood lately!"

As the days went by my boss still yelled, but I was not mad at him. It was a miracle. First came cleansing; then came strength—a strength not my own but God's.

I cannot change what I am deep down inside: only God can. I can only change surface actions. I have a human tendency to idealistically view myself; I thought that I could change my reaction if I was just determined enough. This thinking leads to some great acting but not to a changed and *cured* heart. I may feel that I must add to the finished work of Christ, but when Jesus said,

"It is finished"
JOHN 19:30

He meant it.

Only Jesus lived the Christian life. Only Jesus, in control of our hearts, will enable us to live the Christian life today. Every day that I yielded to Him, I found the Lord was always there. And across these years, the principle that we can live the Christian life with God in control and win against sin has made a tremendous difference in my life.

The Work of the Spirit

Sin has not been eliminated as of the date of the publication of this book!

For the wages of sin is death.
ROMANS 6:23

He will save His people from their sins.
MATTHEW 1:21

One day I walked out to the plant with another engineer named Al. He said, "You seem to be happier lately, and you don't enter into the gripe sessions about the boss any more. What happened?" He took me by surprise. I had no idea that there was any noticeable change since I had asked Christ to take away my anger. I made a feeble effort to explain my quest for help, but as a young Christian, I didn't understand what had happened very clearly myself.

"Can you help my wife and me? We are two miserable people," he said.

My struggle had been very personal to me. I had no interest in getting involved in other people's lives. But his question was a challenge. Since I did research routinely as part of my work, I asked him to give me some time to study and research what had happened to me.

Finally, I had worked up a presentation and told him I was ready. My wife Eva and I invited Al and his wife to come to our house for one evening. When we sat down together, I reminded him that this "change" in my life only happened a few weeks ago. I had no idea how long it would last. Briefly, I told him that several years ago I had asked Jesus to come into my life and save me from my sins. Lately, I had asked Him to cleanse the anger and hate out of my heart, and, as I understood it, He gave me the strength to be kind and tender-hearted on a daily basis.

I told them, "To tell the truth, I feel rather foolish telling you this. It seems as if I should be able to manage my own life, but I can't."

They both had tears in their eyes. They thought it was a wonderful story. I didn't want to get sidetracked from my presentation, so I said, "Let's look at what I have prepared."

I started out in the Garden of Eden. I took him through Moses' problems and the kings and the prophets (I wanted to be thorough). I touched on a few psalms. This took a couple of hours and pretty soon I moved into the New Testament and the gospel. I explained to them that Christ came into this world, and He loved the world so much that He died for us. And then I very generally asked them if they were ready to receive Christ. He said, "You know, I was ready an hour ago." We all prayed rather awkwardly.

I have boiled my presentation down a little bit since then, but Al and Goldie became children of God and the first people I ever introduced to Jesus. Their marriage was healed. They became active in a church and never turned back. I still see Al occasionally. Goldie and Eva are with the Lord.

This experience with Al and Goldie opened up a whole new vista of opportunity for Eva and me that we never knew existed. We developed a hunger to know the Bible and share with other people. We had been going to church regularly and went to Sunday school, but in making preparation to talk with Al, I became aware of huge gaps in my biblical knowledge. The biggest gap was that I didn't know the meaning of sin.

My wife and I began to research into the nature of sin. We found the definition of sin in the dictionary: an offense against God. But we quickly discovered that the subject was broader and deeper than we ever dreamed it would be. In just five Scriptures in the Bible we found over fifty sins listed. (See page 217 and appendix for a more complete list of sins and related Scriptures.)

The Nature of Sin

We grouped the sins against God into four categories in order to understand them (see table 2). The more we studied these lists, the more excited we became! We discovered that if we could eliminate our sins, we would solve most of our own problems and most of the ills of society, including the breakdown of the family, domestic violence, child abuse, rape, murder, violence, political deception, and personal misery. This table is based on Mark 7:21–23, Romans 1:28–31, Galatians 5:19–21, Ephesians 4:25–31, and 2 Timothy 3:1–5.

Table 2: Four Categories of Sins	
1. Sins of the Mind	evil thoughts ingratitude selfish ambition pride deceitfulness covetousness greed lust
2. Sinful Emotions	jealousy anger malice envy bad temper unloving attitude hatred rebellion bitterness
3. Sins of the Mouth	lying backbiting complaining contentiousness disputing blasphemy slandering yelling boasting quarrelsomeness
4. Sins of Behavior	disobedience to parents brutality without self-control stealing adultery murder fornication violence drunkenness revelry

Evil thoughts, lust, and covetousness can lead to premarital sex and adultery. Lying, backbiting, quarreling, anger, and rebellion can lead to brutal violent behavior and even murder. Clearly someone with a brilliant mind who is consumed by greed, selfish ambition, and deception can devise ways to misuse the stock market or government funds.

I looked at these lists as a huge mirror and stepped up to it to see what it would reflect in me. Considering my past problems with my boss, my wife, and my child, it was hard to accept what I saw: evil thoughts, unthankfulness, pride, unforgiveness, deceitfulness, anger, bitterness, rebellion, lying, complaining, yelling, and quarreling. Imagine anyone walking around with all that inside. The simple yet profound statement that the blood of Jesus Christ can wash it all away is exciting! Is it really that simple? It is so easy that it insults our secular intelligence. Everyone, except those who try it, say: "That is much too simple." But the good news about these lists is that we are just a prayer away from help!

One Sunday morning I arrived early at the church where I was to speak. There was only one person in the auditorium. She was in front of the platform, arranging flowers in a basket. Perhaps a dozen varieties of flowers were masterfully arranged so that each flower was displayed at its best, colorful and delicate. The arrangement couldn't have been more beautiful.

My mind raced back to my boyhood. I could see my mother in her flower gardens. She loved to raise many varieties of flowers. In those days, all I could see was flower beds that needed weeding. My mother could see magnificent baskets of masterfully arranged flowers gracing the platform of our church. Every Sunday during flower season, I had to share the back seat of the car with those bouquets. Mom was so excited at the chance to display God's magnificent creation for the praise and adoration of the Creator.

With my mother in mind, I approached the platform and said to the lady, "You sure have done a beautiful job arranging these flowers."

She turned around. I saw an angry-looking woman who growled, "I do it every Sunday. I am stuck with this job. No one else will do it. I'm sick and tired of getting up early enough to be the first one here." She wasn't really talking to me. She was venting an angry, rebellious spirit. She sputtered on to remark that no one appreciated her work.

"Who are you?" she asked, suddenly realizing that she was talking to a stranger. "I'm the visiting speaker," I replied. "Oh," she gasped, "Oh. Welcome to our church." It was an awkward, embarrassing moment for both of us. The mood of the moment didn't fit with the beauty of the flowers and the fragrance in the air.

Later, from the platform, I noticed the same lady. She seemed radiant and cheerful; a note in the bulletin gave her credit for the flowers. Even though she was deceptively charming, she was still suffering from the consequences of sin and didn't know it.

If she were to stand before the list of sins, she would need to check off anger, rebellion, deception. If she would repent and ask God to clean up her heart, she would be able to rejoice and enjoy the privilege of meeting with the Lord alone on Sunday mornings as she worships in His presence by working with the beautiful, fragrant flowers that He created.

What a pity to let sin steal away such a privilege when cleansing of the heart is just a prayer away.

The Bible cautions us not to kid ourselves:

He who covers his sins will not prosper,
but whoever confesses and forsakes them will have mercy.
PROVERBS 28:13

61

If you aren't going to call the list in this chapter sin, then you will look to the world around you for the cause and the solution for items on the list. But if it is sin, then you are looking at the simplest problem in the world to solve. You have the resources of the Creator of the world to help you. There is a supernatural cure for everyone. We don't have to avoid the problem or run away to try to get relief:

> **If we confess our sins,**
> **He is faithful and just to forgive us our sins**
> **and to cleanse us from all unrighteousness.**
> 1 JOHN 1:9

(See appendix for a more complete list of sins and related Scriptures.)

CHAPTER 5

Why Don't You Just Concentrate on the Positive?

Thought Starter

Is it difficult to deal with the negative in your life?

♦

**Walk in the Spirit,
and you shall not fulfill the lust of the flesh.**
GALATIANS 5:16

The Positive of the Negative

My good friend Dick Andrews is a dentist. One day when I went to his office as a patient, I was startled to see him approach me with his hands in rubber gloves and a surgical mask covering his face.

"Are you going to operate?" I asked.

Through the mask he mumbled, "With the advent of AIDS all dentists have adopted gloves and masks as routine protection." Dick proceeded to see if he could find some trouble in my mouth. By the time he did some mysterious poking around, and his dental hygienist got through polishing my teeth, I walked out of there with gleaming, clean, healthy teeth. They looked for problems, and it was positive that he dealt with the negative.

The physician also deals with negatives, yet he is one of the most respected people in the community. The way he helps us is to look for trouble and fix it. I experienced this in high school when I injured my knee while playing basketball. It was badly swollen and just barely fit into my pants leg. I had to keep it bent to ease the pain. I hobbled into the team physician's office on crutches. He said, "You have a bad knee." He didn't even mention my good knee or the rest of my healthy body. (Is that negative?)

He said, "Stretch your leg out on this table," and ignored the fact that this caused me excruciating pain. He began to thump my knee, asking me where it hurt the most. When he found that spot, he thumped it some more to be sure. Then he smiled, "We will need to lance it. This will hurt." Sweat poured out all over my body from the pain. Then he plunged a knife into my swollen knee. Lots of nasty stuff poured out. I had never felt such pain before! But my knee did get better.

It was positive that he dealt with the negative.

The physician and the dentist are members of professions we hold in high esteem. Yet, their focus is on finding trouble in the body: "You have two cavities." "You have an abscess in your knee."

The comforting side of their professions is that when they find out what is wrong, they proceed to fix it. They can only help us as they deal with the negative.

Actually, much of society focuses on correcting or preventing the negative: firemen, police, auto mechanics, physicians, lawyers, dentists, laboratories, and many others. You can imagine the results if a fireman ignored a fire or a doctor only wanted to focus on my good leg. Even in the field of counseling we usually study the problems of clients; we don't spend a lot of time studying happy, contented people. In sports, if you want to be good, you locate a coach who will study what you are doing wrong so you can eliminate that flaw in your performance. So it is with our spiritual lives: we need to deal with the negative.

The psalmist prayed:

> Search me, O God, and know my heart;
> try me, and know my anxieties;

> **and see if there is any wicked way in me,**
> **and lead me in the way everlasting.**
> PSALMS 139:23–24

In order to be healthy, spiritually speaking, we also need to look for trouble, a sinful condition in the body, so it can be fixed. The Bible says:

> **Walk in the Spirit,**
> **and you shall not fulfill the lust of the flesh.**
> GALATIANS 5:16

Filled with the Spirit or Filled with Sin

While my wife and I were researching the subject of sin we also discovered lists that describe the fruit of the Spirit. Look at Table 3 on the next page for the differences in living while being filled with the Spirit and in living a "normal" life with sin in control.

These are based on Mark 7:21–23, Romans 1:28–31, Galatians 5:19–21, Ephesians 4:25–31, and 2 Timothy 3:1–5.

Most people would agree that walking in the Spirit is a superior way to live, but, realistically, a miracle is needed to actually live this way. Fortunately, the power to walk in the Spirit comes from God. No human beings or circumstances can interrupt your relationship with Him.

We all have a choice. The Bible says:

> **In the past you voluntarily gave your bodies**
> **to the service of vice and wickedness**
> **for the purpose of becoming wicked.**
> **So, now, give yourselves to the purpose of righteousness**
> **for the purpose of becoming really good.**
> ROMANS 6:19, PHILLIPS

Table 3			
Spirit-Controlled Living vs. Sin-Controlled Living			
Spirit-Filled Mind		Sins of the Mind	
forgiveness hope appreciation willingness impartiality	self-control mercy humility thankfulness confidence wisdom faithfulness gratitude	evil thoughts unforgiveness covetousness greed lust arrogance	despiteful pride ingratitude selfish ambition deceitfulness heartless faithless haughty
Spirit-Filled Emotions		Sinful Emotions	
love peace gentle spirit gladness	joy long-suffering kindly spirit patient compassionate	hatred rebellion bitterness envy bad temper	anger unloving attitude jealousy malice rage
Spirit-Filled Mouth		Sins of the Mouth	
truthfulness thankfulness gentle answer encouraging tact	praise timeliness soothing tongue pleasant words	lying complaining yelling contentiousness boasting	gossip slandering disputing backbiting quarrelsomeness blasphemy
Spirit-Filled Behavior		Sins of Behavior	

kindness
righteousness
 	
obedience
goodness
courage
 	
endurance
considerate
	gentleness
	self-control
	
	cooperation
	sincerity
	servant
	
	submissive
	impartial
		fornication
		adultery
		
		drunkenness
		murder
		revelry
		
		insolent
		ruthless
		factions
			brutality
			without
			  self-control
			stealing
			violence
			disobedience to
			  parents
			brawling
			favoritism

If you want to enlarge your knowledge of God's resources, study these verses:

Grace and peace be multiplied to you
in the knowledge of God and of Jesus our Lord,
as His divine power has given to us
all things that pertain to life and godliness,
through the knowledge of Him
who called us by glory and virtue,
by which have been given to us
exceedingly great and precious promises,
that through these
you may be partakers of the divine nature,
having escaped the corruption
that is in the world through lust.

2 PETER 1:2–4

Now may the God of hope
fill you with all joy and peace in believing,
that you may abound in hope
by the power of the Holy Spirit.

ROMANS 15:13

Grace to you and peace from
God our Father and the Lord Jesus Christ.
Blessed be the God and Father of our Lord Jesus Christ,
the Father of mercies and God of all comfort,
who comforts us in all our tribulation,
that we may be able to comfort
those who are in any trouble,
with the comfort with which
we ourselves are comforted by God.

2 CORINTHIANS 1:2–4

Strengthened with all might,
according to His glorious power,
for all patience and longsuffering with joy.
COLOSSIANS 1:11

And may the Lord make you increase and abound
in love to one another and to all,
just as we do to you.
1 THESSALONIANS 3:12

But the wisdom that is from above is first pure,
then peaceable, gentle, willing to yield,
full of mercy and good fruits,
without partiality and without hypocrisy.
Now the fruit of righteousness is
sown in peace by those who make peace.
JAMES 3:17–18

Only God can cleanse us from sin and empower us to walk in the spirit. Good news: we are free to choose.

Look! Do You Want to Drive This Car, or Do You Want Me to Do It?

Therefore let him who thinks he stands
take heed lest he fall.
1 CORINTHIANS 10:12

Throughout life I have tended to resist facing up to my sinful behavior when I was in the middle of doing it. Often, to have my sinful behavior pointed out to me was more distressing than the behavior itself. This graphically happened to me once in a manner that I will never forget.

I was speaking fervently one night on confession and repentance. After the meeting, my wife and I drove a while to our next engagement. We stopped to spend the night in a first-class hotel. We slept on the finest mattress money could buy. In the morning we had baths and used the deodorants that the ads say you should use to promote good will. We had a good breakfast. We started out in our new, air-conditioned car, complete with stereo radio.

Humanly speaking, we had to have a good day, didn't we? According to the sociologists, we had a good secure environment, we were well-educated, challenged, enjoyed good housing, good food, we were clean, and we had money. We had it made, didn't we?

It was a beautiful day and all was friendly until we came to a crossroad leading on to the freeway. I turned toward Detroit, our destination, when my wife said, "Henry, you are going the wrong way."

That remark burned me up. My caustic reply was, "Don't you think I know where Detroit is? Look! Do you want to drive this car, or do you want me to drive this car?"

And away we went in air-conditioned comfort. We still smelled good. We had a good breakfast under our belts, we had nice clothes, the scenery was beautiful, the car was driving smoothly, and *I was furious*. Telling me that I was headed in the wrong direction! I'd lived in this area for years and surely knew my directions! After all, when you feel deeply and certain about something, you ought to stick up for your convictions, shouldn't you? She said nothing. She was to handle the road map and keep us from getting lost.

After a while we came to the first exit. A huge sign with an arrow pointed in the direction we were going. Above the arrow was the word *Chicago*. That was the opposite direction from Detroit.

I have a Ph.D. My training is in the area of evaluating data unemotionally and accurately to produce advice based on the data. This is how I make my living. I get paid for my judgments.

I chose to ignore the sign.

Away we went, in air-conditioned comfort. We came to the next exit, which was some distance from the last one. The sign had a big arrow pointing in our direction, and above the arrow: *Chicago*.

Did you ever get that cold, clammy feeling after you have set someone straight that it's possible that you might be wrong? I felt myself becoming more angry *at my wife* and decided to try one more exit, and away we went.

Can you believe that? You smile, but do you realize that you are smiling at a very sad story? What does this illustrate? The weaknesses and limitations of education. Is it not true that in a fit of anger and stubbornness, all you know can get short-circuited and you can act like a stupid fool?

A brittle, electric silence was in the air. Both of us looked straight ahead and were silent.

The next exit was the same. There was that arrow pointing to Chicago. Would you believe that I decided to try one more exit in order to give me time to figure out how to get to Detroit without turning around.

Have you ever acted like that? You know you are wrong, but, so help you, you are not going to admit it. You do everything you can to avoid admitting you are wrong. That is the way it was with me. You couldn't have dragged me off that freeway with a tow truck!

I shared this story with a close friend for his comments before submitting the manuscript for publication. He told me that I needed to reduce the number of exits that I drove past. He said that one or two would be okay, but passing three exits would stretch my credibility and was out of the question.

He pointed out that, in his opinion, it also insulted the intelligence of the reader.

I gave his suggestion serious thought and decided that his constructive comments were logical and correct. But, over the next few days, I kept thinking, "But it is a true story!" Then it hit me: My behavior only reinforces the lesson! We as Christians tend to underestimate sin's power over our behavior. I kept the original story.

Human emotions can totally disengage our brain, preventing rational behavior and acceptance of the fact that we sin. I have seen this in my own life and in those of my clients.

- ♦ An intelligent man nearly destroyed his marriage and family by repeatedly overworking. He was a wealthy, successful lawyer who didn't need to work at all if he didn't wish.

- ♦ Another client came panting into my office and wearily lowered himself into a chair. He was at least one hundred pounds overweight. He called himself a compulsive eater. He was a physician.

- ♦ A beautiful, frightened lady was clasping and unclasping her hands as she told me how worried she was about AIDS. She was sexually active.

- ♦ An affluent couple anxiously asked me for help with a teenage daughter who was on drugs and was sexually active. Against their better judgment, they had showered her with money, cars, and clothes for years.

- ♦ A skeleton of a young lady looked hopelessly forlorn sitting straight in her chair; she was bulimic and starving herself. She was on the honor roll in school.

I find that I must constantly remind myself, again and again, never to underestimate the power of sin to short-circuit my intelligence.

How do you get turned around when you are headed in the wrong direction? The Bible says:

If we confess our sins,
He is faithful and just to forgive us our sins
and to cleanse us from all unrighteousness.
1 JOHN 1:9

I have learned from the Bible that:

Repentance is a five-step process involving God and you. You proceed in the presence of God:

1. I am wrong; I have sinned.
2. I am sorry.
3. Forgive me.
4. Cleanse me.
5. Empower me.

Why Is It Difficult to Say, "I Am Wrong; I Have Sinned"?

"For everyone practicing evil hates the light
and does not come to the light,
lest his deeds should be exposed."
JOHN 3:20

How do you get turned around when you are headed in the wrong direction? I'm three and a half exits down the road. There are no questions at this point: We are headed in the

73

wrong direction; I blew up at my wife for trying to help; and I even tried to tell her that she was wrong. What to do?

How often do you hear someone say; "I am wrong. I have sinned"? Instead, I hear people declare that they are unhappy, tense, anxious, worried, disappointed, misunderstood, mistrusted, unloved, or under extreme pressure.

Frequently I listen to highly intelligent, competent, educated, successful people say the strangest things, such as:

- ♦ "I blew up," or "I exploded." People say this very sincerely. Of course this never happens. Picture a person who blew up: teeth, bones, eyeballs, arms, legs, body parts flying in all directions.
- ♦ "I broke down." Can you see this quivering, helpless body collapsed in a heap?
- ♦ "I lost my head." Can you picture such an unlikely sight of a headless person groping around?
- ♦ "She gets under my skin." One can accept the presence of a microscopic creature having entered the body, but hardly a full-grown woman.
- ♦ "My blood was boiling." This person is no doubt experiencing some bodily changes, but hardly the condition described here.
- ♦ "I was beside myself." This statement simply defies logic.
- ♦ "He turns me on."
- ♦ "He turns me off."
- ♦ "He burns me up."
- ♦ "He turns me cold."
- ♦ "I am fed up."

My purpose in recording these statements is not to belittle anyone or to treat their reports lightly. These are socially acceptable terms describing bodily changes that we are aware of as we interact with people and respond to the events of the day.

We freely describe ourselves and our problems as being caused by other people. But it is very difficult to say the simple words to God, "I am wrong; I have sinned."

If I say, "I am wrong; I have sinned," I have taken the first step toward a cure.

The big little word is *if.* That word represents a major hurdle because I have a tendency to say things like: "I may have been off base, but I have some good points about me. Haven't I been faithful in teaching biblical principles worldwide? Haven't I worked hard at being a good husband and father? Don't I get some points for providing a good home?"

None of my past history helped at this point.

I am three and one-half exits down the pike and going in the wrong direction. That fact couldn't be side-stepped.

When I share this story of driving down the freeway with audiences, I say, "Sin is 'doing wrong according to God's standard.' What were my sins? Can you help me out?"

Without exception, the ladies in the audience always respond immediately and with the same words: pride, stubbornness, rebellion, impoliteness, anger, and bullheadedness.

I reply, "What are you doing diagnosing me? You are not trained, are you? The point is that it is not that hard to figure out what my sins were and you are quickly and accurately diagnosing my problem."

Clearly I am wrong on two points: the condition "under my skin" and the fact that I am going the wrong direction on the freeway.

It is important to understand that I could acknowledge being wrong on all points without agreeing that I have sinned against God. It is important to comprehend that being wrong and being sinful are not interchangeable words. We must be clear on what we mean by being wrong.

I always ask my audiences after they volunteer the words above, "Are you telling me what you think I want to hear, or do you really believe these words are sins?"

How can an audience diagnose my sins so quickly? All of us are familiar with such behavior.

I have noticed the same process in the consulting room. A counselee seldom has any problem describing someone else's weakness or unacceptable behavior. Their memory also serves them well in recalling past instances when someone mistreated them.

To face personal wrongdoing is a different matter. I seldom hear anyone eagerly volunteering information about their own wrongdoings.

But if it is sin, then there is no human remedy. The cure to the problem involves a miracle, and what must happen goes against our human nature.

Step 1:
I Must Confess in the Presence of God, "I Am Wrong; I Have Sinned."

The Bible tells us how to get turned around:

**If we confess our sins,
He is faithful and just to forgive us our sins
and to cleanse us from all unrighteousness.**

1 JOHN 1:9

I need to agree that I am wrong because I have sinned against God's standard. My words and emotional response to my wife's statement were wrong and sin.

As I was driving down the freeway, I realized I was proud (too proud to admit I was wrong), stubborn, rebellious, impolite, and angry. That's hard to admit. To call this response *sin* is even harder. I tend to turn away from this description of myself. It is embarrassing. We seem to ask, "Isn't there a more palatable explanation?"

The Bible records a midnight conversation between Jesus and Nicodemus, the dean of the theological school. Jesus was explaining why people struggle with guilt. He said:

> "This is the condemnation,
> that the light has come into the world,
> and men loved darkness rather than light,
> because their deeds were evil.
> For everyone practicing evil hates the light
> and does not come to the light,
> lest his deeds should be exposed.
> But he who does the truth comes to the light,
> that his deeds may be clearly seen,
> that they have been done in God."
> JOHN 3:19–21

Hear me! It took me four exits to admit that I'm a bull-headed, stubborn, proud, angry person. I don't like that. And my wife had better not tell me that. But, as a counselor who has spent over fifty years of my life working to help people, I have observed that it is very, very difficult to take the first step toward the cure, which is admitting, "I am wrong."

Isn't it often true that before we get turned around to face the truth, we are way down the road somewhere? We must all submit to the same treatment if we are to be cured.

But I have found that when there is a crisis, it's easy to get preoccupied with the other person's sins. When you think of somebody with whom you're at odds, you can think of all the things that are wrong with him. You can even pray for him, "Oh, God, straighten him out." Face it! We all tend to deny our sins.

I must talk to God about my own sins and admit that simple but difficult point: "I am wrong," regardless of the other person's problems.

Step 2:
I Need to Say in the Presence of God,
"I Am Sorry. I Have Sinned."

Yes, but . . . why is it always so important to always get to tell our side of the story?

If to acknowledge sinful behavior is a struggle, to be sorry about it is more of a struggle. Routinely, people ask for a chance to explain their behavior. Then they proceed to describe external circumstances that explain their behavior, making statements such as:

- ♦ "Lord, I'm mad and angry and bullheaded, but who wouldn't be with a spouse like mine?"
- ♦ "The boss yelled at me, and he didn't have his facts straight."
- ♦ "The kids kept fighting."
- ♦ "You drove me to it."
- ♦ "I haven't been getting enough sleep."
- ♦ "I grew up in a bad neighborhood."
- ♦ "I haven't been feeling well lately."

- ◆ "Let me tell you about the problems my family had."
- ◆ "My parents didn't love or understand me."
- ◆ "Lord, this is the way I am, but you know how hard I've tried to serve you."

Do these statements sound familiar? You see, I can announce that I am wrong, but then I want to blame someone else or some circumstances in my life or my background. Jesus once declared to a group of religious leaders:

> **"You are those who justify yourselves before men,**
> **but God knows your hearts."**
> LUKE 16:15

Human behavior has not changed over recorded history, and this step in repenting is just as difficult today as it was in Jesus' time.

Obviously, you can confess to having done something sinful and not be the least bit sorry. You may even be purposing in your heart to repeat the same behavior. Or you may be sorry you were caught, because you will suffer the consequences of your actions. Other times we can sin and apologize to an individual but leave God completely out of the situation.

The apostle Paul wrote to the Corinthians rebuking them for mixing with idolaters. He describes their response to his first letter:

> Now I rejoice, not that you were made sorry,
> but that your sorrow led to repentance.
> For you were made sorry in a godly manner,
> that you might suffer loss from us in nothing.

For godly sorrow produces repentance to salvation,
not to be regretted;
but the sorrow of the world produces death.
For observe this very thing,
that you sorrowed in a godly manner:
What diligence it produced in you,
what clearing of yourselves,
what indignation, what fear, what vehement desire,
what zeal, what vindication!

2 CORINTHIANS 7:9–11

It's a struggle to come to the place where I can say, "I am wrong. I have sinned. No excuses, no alibis. This is my sin and I mean it. I am sorry, God."

Admitting sinful behavior and expressing sorrow for that behavior is rare. It is a struggle to let go of the reasons why our behavior is someone else's fault.

Step 3:
I Need to Ask in the Presence of God,
"God, Forgive Me of My Sins."

When we finally relinquish our excuses, a strange thing often happens: rather than seeking forgiveness, we want to do penance for our sins. As a result, I hear statements such as these:

- ◆ "Can't you see I am crying?"
- ◆ "Can't you see I'm depressed?"
- ◆ "My self-esteem is destroyed!"
- ◆ "I hate myself."
- ◆ "I am unworthy."
- ◆ "My self-image is battered."

More likely we need to review the good news that Jesus shed His blood for our sins to make the free gift of forgiveness available to us. We just need to receive it.

Let me remind you that this encounter is directly between God and you. Only He can forgive and cleanse sin. The apostle John affirms:

> **If we confess our sins,**
> **He is faithful and just to forgive us our sins**
> **and to cleanse us from all unrighteousness.**
> 1 JOHN 1:9

None of the penance programs will help. His Son shed His blood to make this free gift available to us. I need to accept the cure for my past sin. When we sincerely ask, "God, forgive me of my sins," He does!

Step 4:
I Need to Ask in the Presence of God, "God, Cleanse Me of My Sins."

My sins were pride, stubbornness, rebellion, anger and impoliteness. "Cleanse me" sounds easy. However, I have observed this to be an extremely difficult step for many people, especially talented, educated, self-sufficient, independent people. Our tendency is to put confidence in self-control rather than surrender to God. We say, "Now that I know what the problem is, I'll take charge and fix it," or "Just tell me what I'm supposed to do, and I'll do it."

Sometimes we are still not convinced that we have sinned. We take another try at disciplining ourselves to act the way we think a Christian should act. There is no cure at this time, only the counterfeit appearance of a cure. We keep saying: "There must be *something* I can do?"

Not this time. If it is sin, there is no human remedy. Give it up. You have admitted your sin, expressed sorrow, and asked for forgiveness. Now, receive the cleansing. Be specific about what needs cleansing in your life and know that only God can cleanse you from sin.

Step 5:
I Need to Ask in the Presence of God,
"Empower Me."

This is the toughest step of all. It's not a matter of receiving a boost from God to get us started so we can proceed on our own. This step involves the realization that we will be dependent on God forever, not only to cleanse us from sin, but to empower us to keep His commandments in the future.

Intelligent, competent, successful people find this a hard pill to swallow. Our human nature causes us to resist the necessity for a lifetime dependence on God to correct our tendency to sin. And if it's sin, there is no human cure.

For Christians to try to live the Christian life without total dependence on the Holy Spirit is a contradiction in terms. Anything less is just acting. Paul's words are true:

And my God shall supply all your need
according to His riches in glory by Christ Jesus.
PHILIPPIANS 4:19

Be filled with the Spirit.
EPHESIANS 5:18

Also, Peter said,

"As His divine power has given to us all things that pertain to life and godliness, through the knowledge of Him who called us by glory and virtue."

We want to be self-sufficient and independent. Many people have enough self-control to act the way they choose to act. They can rightly say, "Now that I know what to do, I will act like a Christian." They think they are in total control of their own lives. What they have is only a sad counterfeit that appears to be a cure.

To be clean, forgiven, and renewed is a great relief. Now it is time to turn around.

In my story of driving down the freeway, we were three and one-half exits down the pike. Isn't it amazing how long we will fight the truth? Finally I was ready to reach out to God for help. I had to admit to my proud, rebellious, angry, stubborn spirit. My wife can't help me here. She can't cure me. I must deal with God. I asked God to cleanse my heart, to restore His love, peace, and joy to my heart, to help me face the truth. Guess what? He answered my prayer. Up to that point you could not have dragged me off that freeway. Now the most delightful thought in my mind was to look for the next exit. I am free from the effects of my sins. Happy thought. I could turn around.

"Eva," I said, "we are headed in the wrong direction" *(as if she didn't know.)* "I am sorry. Forgive me." It was now easy to admit the truth.

Soon we came to the next exit. We turned around and drove all the way back. And that is sometimes the trail of repentance; we retrace a lot of steps and make some corrections along the way. There is no other way to start fresh and clean.

Personally, I find that I need to frequently repeat these steps. And the mystery is that one can be determined to be consciously wrong, no matter what, and then, in response to a repentant prayer, be transformed into a person who delights in being consciously right.

The Process of Repentance

I have broken down the term *repentance* into five steps. Actually, as we practice this process daily, these steps merge into a smooth process that is like one step. It's like driving a car. A beginner is conscious of the brake, accelerator, speedometer, side mirror, windows, and rear-view mirror. Gradually all these activities merge into one motion. To confess and repent can be as simple as slowing down for a driver who is committed to driving the speed limit.

My phone rang. On the line was a jubilant client who reported this incident. He was an engineer who was struggling with his temper. He had made a mistake that cost his company a lot of money. The day after it happened his boss called him on the phone and firmly reprimanded him. When he hung up the phone he thanked the Lord for the peace he experienced. Normally, he would have been furious. The phone rang and it was the boss's boss. This boss proceeded to reprimand my client also. As he listened he could feel anger welling up within him. Without interrupting the conversation he repented and when he hung up he was peacefully calm. He called me immediately so we could rejoice together that he had found God's peace that passes understanding. You can repent without interrupting your conversation.

As a young Christian (and even to this day), I was astounded at the reluctance of people (including me) to face up to their sins. To bring up the subject creates an atmosphere of resistance, tension, anxiety, and anger.

You would think that everyone would leap at the chance to be rid of sin. Not so. Usually, people do not seek a real cure to their problems (sins); they just want relief from the consequences of their sins.

I'm not some stranger to this material. I'm the one who is teaching and practicing it. But between conferences, look what happened. I don't always know why it happens; but when it does, I need to call it by its right name: sin. In my case, I not only blew up at my wife, but I also tried to tell her she was wrong! To admit our own sin is very difficult for all of us because sin has a way of short-circuiting our brain.

This word *sin* is seldom heard; it is despised, dreaded, and hated. Newspapers scream daily about problems that fit the definition, but they refuse to call it by the right name. Society doesn't put sin into you; it stirs up what is already there. If it is sin, there is no human remedy.

A supernatural cure for sin is available. I can only experience consistent peace, joy, and love when the Holy Spirit is in control of my life.

It is thought-provoking that we have available a supernatural cure for sin, but the whole subject is resisted and its cure is rejected.

After you have dealt with God concerning your sin, then you must correct the relationship with any person you may have offended. Personalizing steps one, two, and three will help you know how to correct the injured relationship.

CHAPTER 6

Why Is It So Difficult to Walk by a Mirror without Looking at Yourself?

Thought Starter

Is the real you underneath your skin?

◆

"For the LORD does not see as man sees;
for man looks at the outward appearance,
but the LORD looks at the heart."
1 SAMUEL 16:7

"Only take heed to yourself,
and diligently keep yourself [your heart]."
DEUTERONOMY 4:9

Heart Check

When people come into my consulting room, I can see that they have taken time to look nice. However, what I talk about is the part of them you cannot see, the world of thoughts, feelings, and emotions underneath the skin.

Very few of us would think of neglecting our appearance before leaving home. We want to make the image we see reflected in the mirror acceptable to ourselves and to others. We know that others make judgments about us based on our appearance.

Very few people get to see what we see in the mirror in the morning. What people do see is our version of what we want them to see. Some people have more work to do than others.

Multimillion-dollar industries provide products for eye care, ear care, lip care, hair care, body care, and clothing.

As you look in the mirror in the morning, you are vaguely aware of your behavior patterns, thoughts, and reactions. Circumstances and events in your life make you aware of pleasant or unpleasant thoughts and emotions. And as you look in the mirror, you are either pleased or displeased with yourself.

With personal behavior, as with personal appearance, you behave acceptably to particular persons or groups. In their presence, regardless of what they say or do, regardless of the reactions going on underneath the skin, you strive diligently to maintain a pleasant smile, a friendly word, and a congenial manner.

Few people get to see what you see in the mirror, and no one gets to see what goes on underneath your skin except God. The Bible says:

> **Man looks at the outward appearance,**
> **but the LORD looks at the heart.**
> 1 SAMUEL 16:7

If the Lord looks at the heart, then it follows that a checkup of your heart is more critical than an examination of your physical appearance.

I don't like checkups. I usually have a feeling of uneasiness and uncertainty that something bad will come up that I don't know about. When a physician checks your body, he is alert to discover anything that needs correcting.

Heart searching can be as uncomfortable as a physical checkup. But if God looks upon the heart, one needs to be sure of His approval. The psalmist said:

> **Search me, O God, and know my heart;**
> **try me, and know my anxieties;**
> **and see if *there is* any wicked way in me,**
> **and lead me in the way everlasting.**
> PSALMS 139:23–24

When Moses passed the mantle of leadership to Joshua, he said to the people:

"Only take heed to yourself,
and diligently keep yourself [your heart],
lest you forget the things your eyes have seen,
and lest they depart from your heart
all the days of your life."

DEUTERONOMY 4:9

Most of us don't need any urging to look after our personal appearances and personal advantages. We encounter people every day, and their approval or disapproval is face to face and immediate.

A Root of Bitterness Unchecked

It is fairly simple to lose sight of the need for the Lord's approval. The effects of deviating from His standards may not be evident to you and others for a long time. As a result, more and more frequently these days I hear about another "model" couple who, after twenty years of marriage, are getting a divorce.

One such marriage might have been saved if they had heeded this biblical advice:

Looking carefully
lest anyone fall short
of the grace of God;
lest any root of bitterness springing up cause trouble,
and by this many become defiled.

HEBREWS 12:15

I was sure that this couple had a marriage that was grounded solidly on mutual devotion to each other. He had poured twelve years of his life into a service organization. He worked long and sacrificially, and his wife was by his side supporting him. We all admired their commitment and even thought of them as a model couple who put serving the Lord as the top priority in their lives.

Then we heard the chilling news that he had resigned from the organization, was divorcing his wife, and would marry another woman. Everyone was shocked. This model marriage had collapsed. I had a chance to talk to him about the surprise development. He was quick to assure me, however, that there was nothing sudden about it. This break had been coming on for years.

He and his wife encountered conflict from the beginning of their marriage. The first issue was over money; she failed to record checks she had written. The monthly bank statements were consistently different from his checkbook. He brought the matter up repeatedly; she ignored the problem. After a few years he quit trying, but a root of bitterness developed in his heart.

There were other issues. One was a running battle about punctuality. They differed over rules for their two teenagers. Another issue was the level of involvement with their immediate families. These issues had rocked along unresolved for seventeen years.

Strangely enough, they had worked together in creating the impression around friends and associates that they were a happy, cooperative couple. But in reality, skillful deception covered growing bitterness.

Eventually his work on a certain committee placed him next to a rather plain-looking woman. He helped her into her chair, and at the break he served her coffee. Nothing unusual about that. At the next meeting he arrived early, as was his custom. He was the first one there, and the second one, also early, was the woman who had sat next to him. He complimented her on being early. She replied that this was her custom, but when she went to meetings with her husband, they were always late. He remarked that he and his wife had the same problem. She complimented him on his attentiveness, remarking that her husband never paid much attention to such things.

He was given responsibility for producing a report, and she was appointed to help him with research and typing. She was prompt and cooperative. He remarked that he wished his wife would work with him like that. He found himself thinking about this woman frequently. Once, they had lunch together to plan their report. His hand brushed hers and lingered there.

She began telling him about other problems she had involving her husband. He sympathized with her because he, too, had some problems with his wife. After lunch, she took his arm as they walked to her car. He found himself thinking about her in the office, and on an impulse, called her and offered to pick her up for the next committee meeting. After driving her home, they sat in front of her house and chatted a while. He walked her to the door and gave her hand a squeeze as he said good-bye. After the next meeting, they spontaneously kissed, which was an electrifying experience that he hadn't enjoyed for a long time.

What these two people had in common was a root of bitterness. As a result, they had forgotten the sweet times in their marriages, and any grace toward their partners had departed from their hearts. Along with the bitterness, uncontrollable lust flared up. From that point, reason went out the window, and before they recovered, they had broken up two marriages, ruined two careers, and ended up married to each other. They soon found out that they had new conflicts to deal with in each other.

Since then, they have come to their senses, have sought God's forgiveness, and are trying to repair the damage that has been done. They are finding out that they have no good options, but must make the best of a hopeless mess: two successful careers and two marriages had died.

An important lesson to learn is the greater the gap between outward behavior and the condition underneath your skin (hypocrisy) the greater the possibility of deceiving yourself.

The Bible says:

> **But be doers of the word,**
> **and not hearers only, deceiving yourselves.**
> JAMES 1:22

A Checkup for the Heart

What happened? This man and this woman had neglected to check up on their hearts.

A checkup of the heart need not take longer than a checkup of one's outward appearance. Regular checkups will serve you well if you correct what needs attention, but often we will go for weeks or months or even years without checking up on our hearts. Why?

> **"Men loved darkness rather than light,**
> **because their deeds were evil."**
> JOHN 3:19

The following is a brief checkup. It will only take a few minutes:

> **Pursue peace with all people, and holiness,**
> **without which no one will see the Lord:**

looking carefully lest anyone fall short
of the grace of God;
lest any root of bitterness springing up cause trouble,
and by this many become defiled.
HEBREWS 12:14–15

The heart is reflected in a special kind of mirror called the Bible. It says:

If anyone is a hearer of the word and not a doer,
he is like a man observing his natural face in a mirror;
for he observes himself, goes away,
and immediately forgets what kind of man he was.
But he who looks into the perfect law of liberty
and continues in it,
and is not a forgetful hearer
but a doer of the work,
this one will be blessed in what he does.
JAMES 1:23–25

Is there conflict between you and someone else? Perhaps even the person on the other side of the bathroom wall in the morning? Does the conflict disturb you? Are you "gracious" about it? Look carefully!

A Look in the Mirror

If you glanced in a mirror and saw a pimple you would surely look more carefully. A pimple! You don't ignore a pimple! This is an emergency! You would move quickly to get rid of it.

We get the word *gracious* from the word *grace* which generally means "loving acceptance." Look carefully lest you fall short of the grace of God. Are you aware of an ungracious spirit toward a family member, a coworker, or anyone? You still act graciously, sound gracious, but deep down inside you are not gracious. Beware. This is more serious than a pimple.

Is there a root of bitterness lurking in your heart toward the person with whom you are in open or hidden conflict? Are you making an effort to be reconciled?

I see many married couples who were at one time, delighting in each other's presence, filled with admiration and appreciation for one another. Because one or both neglected their hearts, they are now estranged. They have forgotten the sweet fellowship of the past, and goodwill towards one another has left their hearts.

Take another quick look at the mirror that reflects your heart:

> Put off all these: anger, wrath, malice,
> blasphemy, filthy language out of your mouth.
> Do not lie to one another.
> COLOSSIANS 3:8–9

> Put on tender mercies, kindness,
> humbleness of mind, meekness, long-suffering;
> bearing with one another,
> and forgiving one another . . .
> even as Christ forgave you,
> so you also must do.
> COLOSSIANS 3:12–13

A Look in God's Mirror—His Word

The Bible is a mirror that will let you know what to put off or put on. You may or may not want to know. You may or may not want to act on your reflection. You can even act like you have put off what needs putting off, and put on what needs putting on, when that really is not the situation under your skin.

Once I stayed in a lovely apartment with a bathroom that had mirrors on all the walls. At first I was pleased, but very quickly I was stunned. I saw views of my body that I had never seen before, and I didn't like what I saw. The easy solution is to stay away from mirrors. The wise solution is to correct what needs correcting.

A couple came up to me after a speaking engagement to share with me the good news of what had happened to their marriage relationship since they both had begun spiritual checkups. A year earlier they had heard me speak on the subject, and at that time the wife had gotten rid of a load of sin that was ruining her life.

She told me her husband had met another woman in a motel occasionally. The relationship ended. She learned about the situation when her husband and the other woman came to her and admitted they had been together.

She was livid with rage toward the other woman and refused to forgive when the woman pleaded for forgiveness. The wife nursed her rage for six years. Even though she and the other woman were now several thousand miles apart, the thought of the other woman would instantly fill her with rage.

"It was like a rope around my neck," she said. Her rage ruined her appetite, gave her pounding headaches, and often kept her awake. She knew all along that nursing her grudge against the other woman was only punishing herself. But nursing an angry spirit was not evil but pleasurable. But as the Bible says:

> But if you have bitter envy
> and self-seeking in your hearts
> . . . lie [not] against the truth
> . . . [it] is earthly, sensual [self-indulgent], demonic.
> JAMES 3:14–16

At the conference a year earlier, the wife suddenly realized that she was punishing herself because her husband and this other person had sinned. Their sin exposed her own sin. She deposited her six-year burden with the Lord; now she was free and their marriage was better than ever.

Can you imagine being at odds over something year after year in a relationship? It is amazing what a low standard of Christian life many of us will tolerate.

As you leave the bathroom in the morning, your appearance can be very different from when you went in. Likewise, we can behave differently from our feelings. We can feel isolated from others, alone in a crowd, detached from reality, uncomfortable, and ill at ease when people praise us. These conditions result because how we talk and act does not accurately reflect what is going on underneath our skin.

Man looks at the outward appearance. The Lord looks on the heart. What really matters is what the Lord sees. He sees the real person underneath the skin. When we bring the sin in our life to God, He takes it away; and we can actually feel under our skin just as we behave on the outside. This resting and peaceful condition of God's forgiveness gives us tremendous relief from stress and fear.

CHAPTER 7

At What Age Is It Acceptable to Sulk When You Can't Have What You Want?

Thought Starter

Why do adults behave childishly?

◆

**Brethren, if a man is overtaken in any trespass,
you who are spiritual
restore such a one in a spirit of gentleness,
considering yourself lest you also be tempted.**
GALATIANS 6:1

**Where there are envy, strife,
and divisions among you,
are you not carnal and behaving like mere men?**
1 CORINTHIANS 3:3

I was sitting alone in a living room, waiting for the man of the house to appear. Instead, a door opened and in walked a small boy. He walked over to where I was sitting and asked me some pointed questions:

- ♦ "Who are you?"
- ♦ "What do you want here?"
- ♦ "Have you got any children?"
- ♦ "I have a dog. Do you like dogs?"
- ♦ "Do your children have a train like mine?"

I had my mind on the reason for my being there, so these questions were distracting me. I tried to think of some way to get his attention away from me, and all I could think of was to give him my billfold to play with.

Immediately I saw that this decision was a mistake. He began to extract my credit cards and money. I needed to redeem my billfold.

My first approach was to ask him to return it in as nice a voice as possible. "Would you please give me my billfold?"

He replied, "That's my billfold."

A simple, childlike transaction. I had no other choice but to take it away from him. In my mind, I needed to be calm, cool, and collected for my appointment, so I needed to bring this encounter with a three-year-old to a swift conclusion. I retrieved my billfold, put the credit cards and paper money in place, and pocketed the billfold. But my little friend was determined to retrieve "his" billfold. He approached me with a smile on his face and in a pleasant voice, he said, "Please, mister, can I have my billfold back?"

With such a sweet request, I felt quite mean and inconsiderate, but I replied, "No, that's my billfold."

"Can't I please have it back? Please, mister? Please, can I have it back?" he pleaded, still smiling.

I was almost persuaded to give it back to him, but I got a firmer grip on my resolve and said as gently as possible,

"No, you can't have it."

As if by magic, this nice, polite, friendly, little boy turned into someone else. His smile was gone. His eyes became slits, he stomped his feet, his little hands doubled up into fists, and in a shrill voice, he shouted, "I want my billfold!"

I said, "No!"

Then he started to cry. Tears streaming down his cheeks, he looked utterly pathetic.

He wailed, "I want my billfold."

I said, "No!"

Finally, he gave me an ugly look and turned his back on me.

He was pouting. I was getting the silent treatment. He acted as though I were nonexistent.

At that point, his father showed up and the incident with the child was over. Later, I had some free time and began to relive that scene.

Small children have some very effective tools to get what they are after. One tool is to be charming by smiling, reaching out for a hug, or being sweet.

There are two definitions for the word *charm*. One is the expression of genuine pleasure, delight, pleasantry, and gratitude. The other is to deceive and pretend pleasure, delight, pleasantry, and gratitude to allure, entice, captivate. In either case, the behavior is the same; the motive is quite different.

I have parents approach me because their child is five years old and clearly still uses deceptive charm (as the three-year-old who approached me) to get what they are after.

We were having lunch with an elderly couple. Their ten-year-old grandchild approached the table. She was all smiles and charm. With her back to Grandpa and hugging Grandma, I heard her whisper in Grandma's ear, "Grandma, can I have a dollar?"

The grandma said, "No, not now."

Then she turned around with her back to Grandma and gave Grandpa a hug and a kiss and told him she loved him. He was noticeably pleased by her attention. Then she asked him for a dollar. He gladly responded. She gave him another hug and kiss and declared her love for him; she gave Grandma a big smile and was gone.

My three-year-old friend's actions in attempting to acquire my billfold and the ten-year-old's success in charming Grandpa out of a dollar start out as childish self-interest. But this behavior works so well that it often is continued into adult life. At what age is it no longer acceptable to use pretended pleasantry for personal gain? Would you say ten, twenty, or forty years old?

Childish Behavior Isn't Just for Children

At what age is it no longer acceptable to throw a tantrum when you can't have what you want? Would you say ten, twenty, or forty? I was lecturing a man in his forties about being a more considerate husband. He was a college graduate and a successful business man. He nodded, approving of what I was saying, *I thought.*

Suddenly, he stood up and shouted, "I've had enough of this. I don't have to pay for this stuff. I don't need to put up with this lecture!" He wheeled around, opened the door, and left, slamming the door so hard the pictures on the walls moved.

Whew!

What happened?

He had a tantrum.

Ten minutes later, the phone rang. It was him, apologizing for his behavior. This is what psychologists call "regressive behavior:" acting like a five-year-old. Why do we continue such behavior? One reason is that an individual believes it still works. Another reason is that anger and wrath are part of our sinful nature.

At what age is it acceptable to cry when you can't have what you want? Would you say ten, twenty, or forty? A woman sits down for a meeting with me, opens her purse, and takes out a tiny handkerchief. When this happens, I can predict that this woman will cry before the hour is up. Sure enough, I will say something she doesn't like. At that point, an amazing thing happens: she will produce one tear from each eye. Not two tears, but one. This is her signal for me to back away from the subject we are on, or perhaps to let me know that I have said something she doesn't like. It is remarkable how long a tear can be suspended in the corner of her eye, but eventually it will trickle down her cheek. At that point she will whisk it away with a practiced hand.

Let me assure you that I am not referring to tears of sorrow or grief or loneliness or real guilt. I refer to the use of tears as a tool to manipulate others so one can get his or her own way. Why do people continue such behavior into adult life? They do so because it has worked successfully in the past. Another reason is that selfishness is part of our sinful nature.

At what age is it acceptable to pout when you can't have what you want? I talked with a couple struggling with both temper tantrums and pouting. Their large home was the scene of much conflict. He wished she were more orderly; she wished he were less rigid. One day he flew into a rage over her closet, demanding that she get it organized. Then he slammed the door, got into his car, and took off, spinning the wheels of his car as he went.

The silence continued for three days. She pouted in response to his tantrum. She would teach him not to yell at her and make demands she refused to meet. This interaction between them had been going on for many years.

Why do adults sulk when they can't have what they want? Because it worked in the past and it still works for them. Another reason is that anger, rebellion, and selfishness are part of our sinful nature.

Paul wrote to some young Christians that he could not treat them as grown-up spiritual people. He pointed out that they were missing out on the happiness that comes with living lives when Christ is in control. They were missing personality qualities such as:

**Love, joy, peace, longsuffering, kindness,
goodness, faithfulness, gentleness, self-control.**
GALATIANS 5:22

According to the Bible, the only way to actually acquire these qualities as part of your being is to recognize that you don't have them unless God gives them to you. Your part is to allow the Holy Spirit to give you something you don't have.

Carnality

Paul used the word *carnal*. We don't see or hear this word used today. Some modern translations say "worldly," one "babes," another "fleshly." Paul said:

**Where there are envy, strife,
and divisions among you,
are you not carnal and behave like mere men?**
1 CORINTHIANS 3:3

Envy, strife, and divisiveness hinder learning and appreciation of others. The apostle Paul calls them "mere men" rather than "spiritual men."

During a recent series of evangelistic meetings, a man with a beautiful singing voice invited Christ to take control of his life. He began attending a church. They soon discovered his fine voice and called on him to sing for some of the church services. Ironically, I had a counselee with a good voice who attended the same church. He was doing the male solo work until this new believer with the better voice came along. They shared vocal responsibilities. My counselee discovered envy and strife in his heart: he could not enjoy the beauty of this new convert's voice. He deeply resented the music director's decision to use the new singer. Several people who knew the situation sided with the music director. There was carnality, envy, strife, and division in my counselee's heart. There was no point in talking about spiritual life with him. He needed to be reminded of the most basic principles of the Christian life. This talented, successful man needed to be approached as if he were a child who knew nothing about the Lord.

As Paul put it:

> I fed you with milk and not with solid food;
> for until now you were not able to receive it.
>
> 1 CORINTHIANS 3:2

Once Jesus told His disciples:

> "I still have many things to say to you,
> but you cannot bear them now."
>
> JOHN 16:12

Isaiah said to his people:

> "Whom will he teach knowledge?
> And whom will he make to understand the message?
> Those just weaned from milk?
> Those just drawn from the breasts?
> For precept must be upon precept,
> precept upon precept,
> line upon line, line upon line,
> here a little, there a little."
>
> ISAIAH 28:9–10

As children often do, my counselee struggled for a while; he wanted his singing position back. There were some tantrums, some weeping, some pouting. Finally, there was repenting or changing of his mind. Today, he is being blessed by the fine singing voice of his vocal partner. Besides, he is chewing on some solid food.

> If we live in the Spirit,
> let us also walk in the Spirit.
>
> GALATIANS 5:25

In order to develop spiritually, we must recognize any carnality or childish, sinful behavior that continues on into adult life. Once the condition is discovered, only God can cure the situation. He alone can clean our hearts from envy, strife, divisions, pouting, temper tantrums, and deceptive manipulation of others. Then we can move on to the meat of the Christian life.

As Paul said:

> And I, brethren,
> could not speak to you as to spiritual people
> but as to carnal, as to babes in Christ.
> I fed you with milk and not with solid food;
> for until now you were not able to receive it,
> and even now you are still not able;
> for you are still carnal.
> For where there are envy, strife,
> and divisions among you,
> are you not carnal and behaving like mere men?
>
> 1 CORINTHIANS 3:1–3

A Victim of Your Own Behavior

Webster defines *forgive* as, "to grant free pardon, cease to feel resentment against."

What are you to do when you must work together with someone who repeats undesirable behavior over and over again, often deliberately and sadistically? This was my question one summer when I was working with the North American Indian Mission along the spectacular coast of British Columbia. Each year the mission sponsored a summer program, placing college students on many of the beautiful islands scattered along the coast line. The mission would assign a team of four to eight college students to an island for a month. Their job was to make friends with the native Indian islanders, to develop a recreation program for the children and an arts and crafts program for the adults, and to encourage them to attend mission meetings and Bible studies.

The mission had a large ship which cruised up the coast from Vancouver to the southern tip of Alaska. Several seaplanes would regularly meet the ship and fly the teams of students to their assigned islands. My job was to help supervise the teams of students. With a pilot and seaplane I flew from island to island to see how the work was progressing.

I had no experience with seaplanes, but I found it a thrilling experience to take off and to land on the water. After my first landing at one of the islands, the pilot asked me to jump out on the dock and hold the rope which was tied to the pontoon of the plane. Glad to be of help, I stood rope in hand under the wing. When the pilot jumped out of the plane and onto the pontoon, the wing came down and struck me in the head. Boom! I saw stars! The pilot was apologetic, "I'm sorry." I replied, "That's okay."

I walked up to the primitive little village where a team of college students were eager to share with me all the unexpected challenges that had arisen. The little kids were hard to manage. They swore. They had lice in their hair. After advising, encouraging, and praying with the team, I returned to the plane.

I made note that these students would need frequent visits to encourage them and to remind them to depend on the Lord daily for grace, love, patience, and wisdom.

The pilot once again asked me to hold the rope while he got into the plane. I was glad to oblige. He jumped on the pontoon. The wing came down and smacked me in the head. Whack! Again I saw stars!

He said, "I'm so sorry."

I said, "That's okay."

My head was somewhat sore, but I ignored it. There was far too much excitement in taking off over the water and rugged landscape. What was a little bump on the head compared to working with such devoted students and these needy Indian children?

As we flew to the next island, I was mildly annoyed at the pilot. My head throbbed, but the beautiful scenery and the three-foot waves which met us at our next landing absorbed my attention.

The pilot asked me to hop out on the dock and hold the rope while he secured the plane. Again I was happy to oblige. Again I felt useful. I was caught off guard when the wing came down on my head: Bang!

The pilot said, "So sorry."

I said, "That's okay."

I know what you are thinking. Why didn't I just get out from under that wing? The excitement of the landings and launchings, the lovely views and my observations of the Indian culture all added up to forgetting to look out for my head.

On the way up to see the students, I began to wonder how sorry the pilot really was. This was no longer okay! I thought, if this happens again, I will throw him into the ocean!

When we arrived at the village, the students told me that they could not get along with each other. One of the fellows was very messy. He had promised his friends that he would change, but he didn't. I told them to be more forgiving of one another.

The pilot and I walked down to the dock. He asked me to hold the rope while he got into the plane. I was glad to comply. The pilot jumped on the pontoon, the wing came down, and I was nowhere near it. I gloated to myself, "Aha! You missed me!"

As we flew along, I rubbed my head and nursed my mean, nasty thoughts; I half grumbled and half prayed for help. Then it hit me like the wing of a seaplane. I had visited teams of students that had to live with circumstances beyond their control. I advised the students to look to God for love, grace, and peace in their difficulties. They had to be more loving and more forgiving of one another.

In the midst of my anger I remembered the following Scripture:

> **Take heed to yourselves.**
> **If your brother sins against you, rebuke him;**
> **and if he repents, forgive him.**
> **And if he sins against you seven times in a day,**
> **and seven times in a day returns to you,**
> **saying, "I repent,"**
> **you shall forgive him.**
> **And the apostles said to the LORD,**
> **"Increase our faith."**
> LUKE 17:3–5

I thought to myself, *I'm with the apostles. If I am to forgive this character and like it, then something special must happen to me now.*

There I was sitting beside a pilot who was also sacrificially serving the Lord. Yes, I was angry and resentful toward him. And I had said nothing. I argued with myself: "What about this pilot? I don't think he's the least bit sorry! So what? If he isn't going to change, why not get out from under the wing? Not a bad idea! But is it fair for him to do this three times?"

Enough of this kind of thinking, I said to myself. I had struck out on two counts. Why not admit it? First, my heart needed to be cleansed and renewed; my attitude was indefensible! Second, I had failed to confront the pilot. Such behavior was clearly a violation of what Jesus taught.

I admitted to God that my attitude was lousy and that I had failed to communicate with the pilot. I asked Him to forgive me, to cleanse me, and to renew my spirit. The Lord heard my prayer, and my heart was changed right there in that plane. I was the victim of my own behavior.

We approached another island where we would spend the night. The landing was smooth. The pilot asked me to jump on the dock and hold the rope. I was only too glad to comply. I was a wise, knowledgeable veteran. The pilot crawled out of the plane and, as always, jumped on the pontoon. The wing came down and disturbed only air; Brandt's head was not under the wing!

That night under the stars as we sat around a campfire, I told the pilot about my struggle. Jesus says to rebuke someone who sins against you. I assumed I should be gracious about it. "You kept saying you were sorry," I reminded him.

"What I meant was, 'I'm sorry if you're too dumb to get out from under the wing,'" he replied, holding his sides with laughter.

This incident started my thinking. Was he serious? Did he mean that he deliberately jumped on the pontoon, knowing that I stood under the wing and would receive a whack on the head? Was this a typical bush pilot joke that they all played on newcomers? Perhaps he had adopted a popular view that says you learn best by taking the consequences for misbehaving. But shouldn't he at least have instructed me to get out from under the wing when he jumps on the pontoon? Remember:

> "If your brother sins against you, rebuke him;
> and if he repents, forgive him."
>
> LUKE 17:3–4

Did that mean that I should chew him out? Vent my wrath on him? What if he said he had repented but continued his unacceptable behavior?

Another verse will shed some light on these questions:

> Brethren, if a man is overtaken in any trespass,
> you who are spiritual
> restore such a one in a spirit of gentleness,
> considering yourself lest you also be tempted.
>
> GALATIANS 6:1

This verse tells me that if anyone mistreats me, I need to first examine my own heart. I need to be "spiritual" before I approach the other person. What is "spiritual"?

> The fruit of the Spirit is
> love, joy, peace, longsuffering, kindness,
> goodness, faithfulness, gentleness, self-control.
>
> GALATIANS 5:22–23

If I am not spiritual, I need to straighten myself out before I approach the other person. If I qualify, I need to rebuke him; that is, I need to point out the offensive or unacceptable behavior to my brother. His response shouldn't affect my spirit because my spirit is between God and me.

What about the other person's behavior? If he repents, forgive him, that is, grant free pardon and cease to feel resentment against him.

In this instance he did repent. He agreed to warn me when he was about to jump on the pontoon. Obviously, I needed to keep on being "spiritual." His present or future conduct didn't dictate the condition of my heart.

In the future, I could be more alert. I could accept his way of doing things. When he is around the plane, I could be sure not to be under the wing. Occasionally I could remind him to let me know when he was about to jump on the pontoon. Otherwise, I would allow myself to become the victim of my own behavior or lack of behavior.

Rebuke and Forgive

Suppose someone is repentant and still repeats undesirable behavior over and over. Our verse says to rebuke and forgive.

I found myself in this situation with my wife, Jo. Shortly after saying our marriage vows, we learned that some adjustments were necessary.

I was driving, and Jo was sitting next to me when she said, "Henry, would you please not drive so closely to the car in front of us?"

I proceeded to defend my driving style and driving record. "Look, I haven't had an accident in years, and I am in better passing condition when I am close to the next car." She insisted that I was driving too close. We were clearly annoyed at each other.

Finally I saw the light. How selfish of me to ignore her request and not make driving with me more relaxing for her. I agreed to open the distance between our car and the one we were following. But I learned that driving habits are not easily changed. I would unthinkingly lapse into my old habits. Often I would remind myself; if I didn't, Jo surely would. There were some trips when I needed to repent seven times in a day. After weeks of catching myself and Jo rebuking me, I've developed the habit of staying the proper distance from the car in front of me. Occasionally, I need to correct and "walk in the Spirit." She needs to rebuke and forgive.

We had another adjustment to make. Jo had a habit of taking off her glasses and laying them on her lap, a table, a car seat, or any other handy place. They would slide off her lap and disappear, or she would forget where she had left them. She was constantly looking for them.

This was unacceptable to me. I felt something simple could be done to solve the problem. She reluctantly agreed to put them in her purse when she took them off when she was away from home. At home, there were two designated places for them. If I saw her put them down anywhere else, I would remind her on the spot. For a while it was a case of reminding her many times every day. Her response wasn't very friendly, and neither was my response to her response. We both had to repent of our bad attitudes. But the "rebuke/ repent" process worked. It quickly became apparent that knowing where her glasses were was worth the effort on both of our parts.

These adjustments made it clear that we both needed to walk "in the Spirit" and we need to maintain a "rebuke-repent" process to deal with occasional lapses.

I met with a man who came to see me regarding his wife. He had married a door slammer. She would slam the car door as hard as she could. She'd slam the front door, the kitchen cupboard doors, the bedroom doors, the bathroom door, and any other door she needed to close. He would wince whenever she approached a door. He could hardly stand it any more.

"Have you talked to her about it?" I asked.

"No, we have only been married a few months. If I criticize her, it may hurt her self-image. I am trying to encourage her."

I called his attention to Galatians 6:1. No need to be critical. The Lord will help him to be gentle. There is no way for her to know what is in his mind if he doesn't tell her.

When he asked her to close the doors more gently, she was quite willing to comply. She had no idea that this behavior troubled him; he was greatly relieved. She then got up out of her chair and went to the bedroom and slammed the door. She was truly willing to change, but slamming doors was so much of a habit she did it without thinking. She actually needed to repent seven times a day, and he needed to forgive her just as often. But with two of them working together, she changed her behavior in a few weeks. It took two spiritual people who worked together to solve a problem.

What do you do about unacceptable behavior that may be repeated seven times in a day? *First, you walk in the Spirit.* It is a fallacy to blame someone else's behavior for your anger or resentment. This is a sin. Your spirit involves God and you. *Second, there needs to be a change of behavior.* You need to rebuke, that is, describe the unacceptable behavior. *Third, you need to deal with the person's response.* If there is repentance, you forgive. If there is improvement, you praise. But what if there is no change? What then?

What should your response be if someone says they are sorry, but repeats the same behavior day in and day out? You may need to conclude that "I am sorry" is meaningless. What you do about it depends on the relationship. Are you dealing with a child, a parent, your partner, a friend, an employee? Certainly, you need to walk in the Spirit. *Fourth, depending on the relationship, you may need to reward, praise, punish, remind, train, or even fire someone.*

In my case, I simply needed to get out from under the wing. My assignment to hold a rope provided me with some insight into my own heart and the chance to learn a new lesson about communication and forgiveness (and how to avoid a bump on the head!).

CHAPTER 8

I Need to Forgive Those Soldiers

Thought Starter

Has a grudge ever helped you?

◆

**Bearing with one another,
and forgiving one another,
if anyone has a complaint [grudge] against another;
even as Christ forgave you,
so you also must do.**
COLOSSIANS 3:13

A bloody civil war raged in Uganda. There were shortages of food, water, vehicles, gasoline, and clothing. The roads had potholes the size of a car. Everywhere we looked there were ugly war machines: tanks, trucks, artillery. We had to pass through frequent checkpoints manned by armed teenaged soldiers. We were stopped twelve times while driving the twenty-five miles from the Entebbe airport to the capital city of Kampala. Each checkpoint made us open our bags for inspection.

The next day, we were to travel to another city where I was scheduled to address a meeting. Sam, my driver, had been scouring in vain to find some gasoline for our vehicle. We were three hours late when Sam finally came to me to say he found some gas for $30 per gallon. We needed fifteen gallons or $450 worth.

I questioned our going. Who would wait for a foreign speaker who is three hours late? Sam convinced me we should go. It was a slow, bumpy ride and there were more road blocks manned by unfriendly soldiers. We arrived at the meeting place, which was packed with people. It was hot and humid; the air in the room was almost unbearable.

I sat on the platform, looking out at the audience. I knew most of them were hungry. They were shabbily dressed, and I knew no one in this audience had stood in front of a closet packed full of clothes and wondered what to wear. What could I say to these people? I knew that many of them had suffered the death of family members. Many of their families were scattered, some having fled into the forest to avoid being mowed down by hostile gunfire. I prayed silently, "Lord, I don't know what to say to these people. Help me."

The only thought that came to me was:

But the fruit of the Spirit is love, joy, peace, longsuffering, kindness, goodness, faithfulness, gentleness, self control. Against such there is no law.
Galatians 5:22–23

I told them I believed that each one of them could have all they wanted of a free gift. The gift was the fruit of the Spirit. It was freely available to my people, and I believed it was also available to them.

After the meeting, a raggedly-dressed man approached me. He said I seemed uncertain about my message. He reassured me that the fruit of the Spirit was available in Uganda, but I had left an important condition out of my message. He asked me if I would take the time to come to his home. He would like to tell me his story.

As we walked down a dusty road in the intense heat, he pointed to a large house, with perhaps five or six bedrooms, up in the hills. "That was my house," he said, "but Idi Amin's soldiers came one day and took it as headquarters for his army. My family had to flee and today they are in the forest. I had a Mercedes Benz parked in front of my clothing store.

One day the soldiers came and took my car. Then they took my store."

We had been walking on this dusty road lined with mud-walled huts with thatched roofs. We came to one and he indicated that this was where he lived. We entered it: one dark room, dirt floor, and a box on the floor. He motioned me to sit on the box. He sat on the other end of it and continued his story.

"I would sit in my chair and work myself into a frenzy over the soldiers who took my car, my business, my house, and scattered my family. I was consumed with hatred, bitterness, and anger.

"When I was forced to leave my house, I took along a chair. I had a cow, also, which needed some fly spray. I traded my chair for the fly spray, but my cow died. I also had a goat and traded my goat for some seeds to plant a garden. But it didn't rain, so my garden failed. Now I have no car, no business, no house, no family, no chair, no cow, no goat, no garden.

"One day, as I sat on this box and rehearsed all of this, I thought I would burst with hatred and animosity. A man came to my door in the middle of this situation. He said he was a missionary and had come to tell me that God loved me. That's all I heard. 'God loves me?' I exploded. 'Do you know what has happened to me?'

"In a rage, I picked that man up and threw him out of my house. God loves me! I was so mad I could hardly contain myself! To my surprise, the man got up and came back in. I was startled at his boldness. He said he had come to tell me about Jesus and would like to continue. He told me, 'God loves you so much that He gave His own Son to die for you. If you ask Him, He will come into your life and change your heart.'

"At that moment I was so furious I hardly knew what to do with myself. Then suddenly, what this man said gave me some hope. I needed something, so I asked Jesus to come into my life right then. He did."

Love and Forgiveness

"Now I come to the part of my story that has to do with your message. I told you that something was missing.

"When I asked Jesus to come into my life, I could still see my home occupied by soldiers, my Mercedes Benz being driven by soldiers, my business ruined, my family scattered, with no garden and wondering how to survive. My heart was still filled with animosity toward those soldiers. My new friend read me a Bible verse intended for children of God:

> **For if you forgive men their trespasses,**
> **your heavenly Father will also forgive you.**
> **But if you do not forgive men their trespasses,**
> **neither will your Father forgive your trespasses.**
> MATTHEW 6:14–15

"A shaft of light into utter darkness! I needed to forgive those soldiers. I needed to love them. Suddenly I wanted to love them. I opened my heart and poured out all the hate and anger and bitterness that I had stored up there. All I wanted was the fruit of the Spirit in my heart.

"You are right," he said. "We can have all we want for free. But you must meet God's terms. You must forgive men their trespasses."

My new friend said he was the richest man in Uganda. He had been released from the unbearable load of sin (hate, anger, bitterness) and now was basking in the unlimited wealth of the fruit of the Spirit. He reminded me that God is the source of the fruit of the Spirit. As we parted, I promised him that I would share his story with others.

As I walked away, I remembered a man who had never paid me back some money I had lent him. I had nursed a grudge against him for a long time. (Webster's defines *grudge* as a "cherished ill will with deep resentment at a real or imagined slight.") I, too, had to release that grudge; I did after a struggle similar to my new friend's struggle. The man still owed me the money, but what a difference to love a debtor instead of hating him.

My new friend faced greater problems than most of us can imagine. How foolish it was to add the pain resulting from hate, anger, and bitterness when he could change them for peace, joy, love, kindness, and forgiveness.

I can be just as angry over my little problems as my friend could be over his big ones. The fact that a man did not pay me back my money did not determine what was in my heart. His decision only revealed the condition of my heart. The money issue is between the man and me. The condition of my heart is between God and me.

I will never forget the man from Uganda who took the time to minister to me. In order for any of us to experience the fruit of the Spirit, we must let go of our pet grudges. For him it meant forgiving those unnamed soldiers. For me it was forgiving someone who had failed to repay a debt owed to me.

Many people who come to me for help hold longstanding grudges. Years ago I naively thought that it would be music to their ears to hear that they could let them go and released from the ill will and animosity that gripped their hearts. I have learned that for many people, the older a grudge (or a pet peeve) gets, the more precious it becomes, like a family heirloom. A person can carefully nurture a grudge. It may be toward someone several thousand miles away. You can recall such a grudge when you have an odd moment to reminisce, work yourself into a frenzy, then carefully put it aside until you have another off moment. To give up that grudge would be a sacrifice rather than release.

Remember, circumstances that come into our lives show us what is in our hearts.

> **Love your enemies,**
> **bless those who curse you,**
> **do good to those who hate you,**
> **and pray for those who spitefully use you**
> **and persecute you.**
> MATTHEW 5:44

How Can I Forgive?

At another conference, in Zimbabwe, I told the audience the story of the Ugandan businessman who had lost everything when Idi Amin's soldiers had seized his possessions and his family had to flee to the forests. This businessman had peace in his heart only after he had forgiven the soldiers.

After my morning address, I received a note requesting a private meeting. To my surprise, I found myself sitting across from a couple from Uganda who had been urged by some friends to attend this conference. Deeply disturbed by a tragedy in their own lives, the couple had listened intently to the story of my Ugandan friend.

As they sat before me, they told me how they had struggled to keep their business going in spite of the turbulence of Uganda's last twenty years.

Then one day during the bloody reign of Idi Amin, they received a note stating their twenty-six-year-old son had been kidnaped and was being held for ransom. The parents did nothing for a few days, and then received a note threatening that their son would be killed if they did not pay the ransom.

The couple sought legal advice and consulted with the proper government authorities. They were advised to resist payment. Then came another note. This was the final warning. If payment was not made immediately, their son would be tortured and killed. As they agonized over what to do, they received a note stating that their son was dead. Grief stricken, the father tried to locate the body.

Finally he found someone who, for a price, would lead him to his son's body. When he arrived at the appointed place late one night, he was seized by a group of soldiers and taken to a prison. In the same cell that had held his son, they stripped him to the waist and made him face a wall. With a whip made of leather strips, they cut his back to ribbons. They loaded him into the back of a pickup truck and dropped him off on a street corner. They shouted at him that if he ever tried to locate his son again, he would be killed.

Two years had passed. The couple had suffered bitter, deep hatred toward unknown soldiers who had murdered their son and beaten the father until he was unable to lie on his back for two months. They could no longer enjoy success in business, a spacious home in the country, and a happy family life. Now each day was filled with sorrow, hatred, and thoughts of revenge. The story of the Ugandan businessman had disturbed them; they wanted to know if I believed they were wrong to treasure their misery and keep their hatred alive. It seemed to them that resentment was normal and proper. To forgive the soldiers seemed to them to be inappropriate and disloyal to the memory of their son.

124

What could I say? Theirs was a tragic story. Surely they had the option to choose their own approach to the cruel, heartless event that had clouded their lives. The problem was so far removed from my own life experiences that it seemed almost from another world. I required more wisdom than I possessed. "God, help me," I quietly prayed.

We sat in silence in a dimly lit room. I couldn't think of anything to say to the dear couple. The woman's eyes were filled with tears. The gentleman sat with his elbows on his knees and both hands covering his face. The wife whispered, "It would be a relief to put this behind us and get on with the future." "Yes, it would," he replied. "Can you help us?"

How could I help? I leaned back in my chair and thought to myself, "What would the Ugandan businessman who had lost everything say to them right now? I believe he would have said:

> "Let all bitterness, wrath, anger, clamor,
> and evil speaking be put away from you,
> with all malice.
> And be kind to one another,
> tenderhearted, forgiving one another,
> just as God in Christ forgave you."
> EPHESIANS 4:31–32

Murder and merciless beatings are heinous deeds. Many friends and associates had assured them that revenge, anger, and hatred were natural responses. To think of being kind and tenderhearted and forgiving was beyond consideration.

Forgiveness Heals!

As the three of us struggled in that dark room in Zimbabwe, it seemed to me that there was another presence in the room.

God was there telling me to gently urge this dear couple to let go of their hostile spirit and let Him cleanse their hearts. He would give them a kind, tender, forgiving spirit. Jesus would say:

> "But I say to you,
> love your enemies,
> bless those who curse you,
> do good to those who hate you,
> and pray for those who spitefully use you
> and persecute you."
> MATTHEW 5:44

I suggested that they needed to pray for such a change of heart. After a long silence, the man said in a trembling voice, "I am ready." His wife said, "So am I."

The three of us knelt by the bed in that quiet room. I have never heard such moving prayers. We stood up and embraced each other with tears of supernatural joy streaming down our cheeks.

The next day the man and his wife stood before the entire gathering. He told the group that he and his wife were leaving a heavy burden behind and looking forward to a new life in the future. I knew what he meant.

God's children have full access to the limitless supply of the fruit of His Spirit: love, joy, peace, longsuffering, kindness, goodness, faithfulness, gentleness, and self-control. Isn't it odd, therefore, that we should ever choose hatred, resentment, or anger, not over the great tragedies of life, but more often, over the small grievances of daily living?

Inevitably, my response is involved in a deed that needs my forgiveness. This response forces me into the need for personal examination. If there is anger, hatred, the desire for revenge, or physical attack, then I must deal *with me* before I can deal with the offense. I can get so preoccupied with the offense, I fail to recognize my own need. Jesus once advised a multitude:

"Why do you look at the speck in your brother's eye,
but do not consider the plank in your own eye?
. . . Hypocrite!
First remove the plank from your own eye,
and then you will see clearly
to remove the speck out of your brother's eye."

MATTHEW 7:3, 5

To forgive and be forgiven go hand in hand. Therefore, when someone trespasses against us, we usually must deal with our own sins as well as with the other person.

But people want to know when it is acceptable not to forgive. We are confronted on all sides with stories of physical abuse, sexual abuse, rape, unfaithfulness, stealing, suffering, swindling. The list is long. Is no one entitled to nurse resentment, bitterness, and to withhold forgiveness? Why should we forgive such treatment? The answer is clear.

The Ugandan couple experienced a miraculous cure when they released their anger and bitterness. Forgiveness freed them from the non-productive and destructive emotions which chained them and enslaved them to the object of their anger. They found that forgiveness was the foundation of good mental health.

These things I have spoken to you,
that in Me you may have peace.
In the world you will have tribulation;
but be of good cheer,
I have overcome the world.

JOHN 16:33

127

I Hate Pain!

For this day is holy to our LORD.
Do not sorrow,
for the joy of the LORD is your strength.
NEHEMIAH 8:10

This is the day which the LORD has made;
we will rejoice and be glad in it.
PSALMS 118:24

Several years ago I had some difficulty digesting one of my wife's typical, sumptuous, delicious Christmas dinners. The discomfort lasted several days, and a physician neighbor urged me to go to the hospital the next morning for a blood test.

A short time after the examination, he came into the waiting room and told me my appendix had to come out immediately. My reply was: "Hey, let's cool it and think it over for a few days. I know you need the work, but let's slow down here." He assured me that he was serious. I was to go at once to a hospital room, and he would operate as soon as I could be prepared for surgery. Prior to this I had only been hospitalized for two days to give an injured knee some rest.

The next thing I knew I awoke from the effects of the anesthesia. For two days my total attention was focused on me and my excruciating, horrible, unendurable pain! The pain was so bad that I would think carefully before even moving a hand! All the muscles in my body would become tense, anticipating another knife-stabbing pain.

The first day after surgery, a nurse insisted that I get out of bed and take a few steps.

"You are kidding," I said, "There is no way you'll get me to do that!"

Unyielding, she firmly made me get up. The pain was incredible. A cold sweat all over my body added to my amazing, unbelievable discomfort. I would cringe with every move. To take one more step seemed inconceivable. She claimed that to move around was a short cut to healing and to the elimination of future extended pain. But returning to my bed was beyond consideration. I told the nurse that I would just remain standing in the middle of the room if it was okay with her. Remaining firm, she forced me back into bed. Exhausted, all I could concentrate on was my painful body bathed in sweat. All I wanted was a pill to rescue me from my misery.

Peace in the Midst of the Pain

During the second night, when darkness enveloped the room, it was a lonely, forsaken place indeed. I'm sure there were no audible voices in that room and I have no idea what time it was, but it was as though I heard a voice that said: "Why do you lay there suffering alone when I laid down my life to be with you, to give you my peace and joy and comfort?"

For the first time in two days, my mind was focused on something other than my own misery.

As I lay there in the hospital bed, I began thinking that for more than a quarter of a century I had traveled the world, telling people about Jesus. I had taught people that He gave His life so that He could come into our lives and be with us, that He promised to comfort us, and that He promised to give us peace and joy. I had taught this all those years, and now, there I lay, all alone, bathed in sweat, my muscles in knots, dreading every new second of my miserable life. Surely this was not peace or joy. This was not fellowship with the Lord.

It hit me: for two days and a night I had not given a thought toward the Lord. I had not even considered that peace and joy were possible with the presence of this pain I felt. I had been told that the discomfort would last for two weeks. Surely comfort and peace meant the absence of pain; they had nothing to do with God! I was shocked at my own thinking!

Why was I two days late in coming to God? Well, this was the first physically painful experience in my life that I couldn't handle. I never related pain with peace because I had never had to in the past. I might have hit my finger with a hammer or had a sore knee, but that was the worst that had happened to me physically.

I like Billy Graham's definition of joy: "Joy is not gush: joy is not jolliness. Joy is simply perfect acquiescence in God's will, because the soul delights itself in God."[1]

I began to pray, "Lord, I'm sorry I've turned my back on You. I've assumed that comfort and peace depended on finding a painless position in bed or by swallowing a pill. Forgive me, Lord. I thought I was dependent on You, but here I am trying to be self-sufficient. If your Word is true, then I repent. Comfort me. Restore Your peace and joy."

I was amazed that I felt my muscles relax. The sweating ceased. Soon I fell asleep.

The next morning was great. My first waking sensation was a stab of pain. I welcomed it. The dread was gone. My body was relaxed. I worked my way out of bed alone, amazed and pleased to discover that a body at peace can take a lot of pain.

I went home the fifth day and was told that the pain would gradually diminish over a period of two weeks. The presence of a wife who was there twenty-four hours a day was a great treasure. Savoring the smells of my wife's cooking was delightful, and eating that delicious food was pleasurable as I looked out at the ocean view. Her presence by my side in the hospital and at home was satisfying beyond description. The sympathy and love shown by Betty, Leroy, Lois, Bob, and Jayne are treasures one cannot buy. Phone calls from all over the country and a stack of cards six inches high were a delight. A warm, friendly, compassionate surgeon, a nurse (actually a very nice person), and aides made up a presence to be appreciated beyond words. What more could one ask for? Yet none of these wonderful privileges were a substitute for God's comforting presence in my heart.

How does God fill your body with comfort and peace and joy in the presence of pain? I don't know how He does it. But Jesus proved to me that His own words are true:

> **Come to Me,**
> **all you who labor and are heavy laden,**
> **and I will give you rest.**
> MATTHEW 11:28

He was there all the time, but for two days I depended solely on my bed, water, pills, the presence of skilled medical personnel, and visits by my wife and friends.

You would think that Jesus would say, "You turned your back on Me; now I'll turn my back on you. It's only fair. Call on Me in a few more days after I've nursed My hurt feelings for a while."

No, He kept His word. He was there when I called.

Why did I have to go through the pain of an operation? Why do we even have pain in the world? I don't have all the answers to that question. I just know that when we have circumstances that are difficult, God has provided a way to have peace in the middle of pain.

Two weeks after I came home from the hospital, my wife had a sudden, strange attack. She crawled into bed and stayed there a full day. Our friend Betty came down from her apartment to help. My wife said to us, "Go out of the room and leave me alone. Your presence bothers me." Betty and I just looked at each other. I hobbled out of the room wondering what to do; this wasn't the predictably pleasant Eva that we knew. Something had to be drastically wrong. We called in our doctor neighbor, and he confirmed that something was seriously wrong.

Two days later, after Eva had been to a hospital for some tests, our beloved surgeon called on us in our home: "I'll level with you," he said gravely. "You have an abdominal tumor, Eva. Very likely it is malignant. We must operate at once."

The Fundamentals of Faith

He left. We sat silently, stunned. Cancer! How can this be? Eva had never been sick. Neither one of us said it, but we both knew we could be staring a painful death in the face. Now my new hospital experience with Jesus served us well.

Death? Eva?

We decided to review the fundamentals of our faith before the operation. There was no need for her to make the mistake of ignoring God's help as I did.

Fundamental #1: The Other Side of Death Is Heaven.

> [Jesus said:] "I go to prepare a place for you.
> And if I go and prepare a place for you,
> I will come again and receive you to Myself;
> that where I am, there you may be also."
>
> JOHN 14:2–3

For the Christian, the other side of death is heaven. It is a good idea to drop that thought into your mind before stressful conditions swirl around you. I only advise this process for the Christian, however; for the non-Christian, thinking about the other side of death will possibly increase stressful feelings.

Fundamental #2: God Will Provide as Much Strength as You Need in a Day.

> Then he said to them,
> "Go your way,
> eat the fat, drink the sweet, and send portions
> to those for whom nothing is prepared;
> for this day is holy to our LORD.
> Do not sorrow,
> for the joy of the LORD is your strength.
> NEHEMIAH 8:10

This was a precious promise given to the Israelites as Nehemiah repaired the wall and gates around Jerusalem. The project was completed in spite of continuous harassment from Israel's enemies and resistance and criticism from many of his own people. We rested our meager faith on this promise. There would be as much strength as needed in a day, enough to joyfully endure the daily demand.

Fundamental #3: God Provides the Greatest Comfort Available.

> [The] God of all comfort . . .
> comforts us in all our tribulation,
> that we may be able to comfort
> those who are in any trouble,

**with the comfort with which
we ourselves are comforted by God.
For as the sufferings of Christ abound in us,
so our consolation also abounds through Christ.**

2 CORINTHIANS 1:3–5

We needed to look to God for comfort, which is not the same as the reassurance that comes from being surrounded by skilled professionals, loving family and friends, good equipment, and medicine. We deeply appreciated human help, but humans could not do what only God could do.

As we prepared to take my wife to the hospital, she decided not to trust her memory. She wrote these verses on three-by-five cards and took them with her:

As your days, so shall your strength be.

DEUTERONOMY 33:25

**For as the sufferings of Christ abound in us,
so our consolation also abounds through Christ.**

2 CORINTHIANS 1:5

**I have suffered the loss of all things . . .
that I may know Him and
the power of His resurrection,
and the fellowship of His sufferings,
being conformed to His death.**

PHILIPPIANS 3:10

**Let the peace of God rule in your hearts . . .
and be thankful.**

COLOSSIANS 3:15

The operation was over. She had a tube in her nose and down into her stomach. Another tube was attached to the abdominal area. Another one led to a bottle suspended above her head and off to one side. Her operation made mine look like no operation! Yet she seemed to be enveloped in a cocoon of peace. The doctors, nurses, her roommate, and her visitors all noticed it and marveled. Her successful recovery was a serene, peaceful scene in the presence of excruciating pain.

What a contrast to my miserable, unhappy, complaining, self-centered response to the first two days after a minor operation. If you prefer my kind of response, God will honor your choice. On the other hand, He will give you peace and joy if you let Him.

How does God do it? He doesn't explain. But by a step of faith, Eva found that she could have peace and joy in her heart when her body was afflicted with seemingly unbearable pain.

When I was a young engineer and struggling to understand what the Christian life was all about, I fell in love with this Bible verse:

> **I know whom I have believed**
> **and am persuaded that He is able to keep**
> **what I have committed to Him**
> **until that day.**
> 2 TIMOTHY 1:12

Thirty-five years later, in my wife's hospital room, we knew that we could trust biblical principles. In this crisis, we were not two desperate people thumbing through an unfamiliar book to learn about a strange God. Rather, we were two people reviewing Bible verses and reaching out to a familiar Friend we had tried to follow for thirty-five years.

Billy Graham said it very well:

Mount Everest was never climbed in a day. Those who attempt to climb its treacherous slopes spend months, even years, in training and practice. Each small mountain conquered prepares one for a higher mountain and a tough climb ahead.

So, too, the best preparation for tough times are the little difficulties and how we react to them ... You and I are called upon to learn what it means to trust God in every circumstance, and to live for Him no matter what comes our way.

We must think more clearly about suffering and rearrange our priorities so that when Armageddon comes, we will not be taken by surprise or be unprepared. Like Joseph storing up grain for the years of famine that lay ahead, may we store up the truths of God's Word in our hearts as much as possible, so we are prepared for whatever suffering we are called upon to endure.

As an army officer once said, "Weather in war is always favorable if you know how to use it."[2]

Many of us find life hard and full of pain. We cannot avoid these things; but we should not allow our harsh experiences to deaden our sensibilities and to make us stoical or sour. The true problem of living is to keep our hearts sweet and gentle in the hardest conditions and experience.[3]

I am sure that the loving Lord scheduled my operation just before my wife's so that I could appreciate and understand the pain that she experienced.

I also learned that my natural tendency in an unfamiliar traumatic situation was to look for peace after the end of the difficult circumstances, rather than obtain peace from God in the middle of the circumstances. When my wife and I focused on the Lord before and after her surgery, we both found that there was a world of difference in the peace in our hearts.

Based on my own personal experience, I recommend that everyone seek God *before* any operation or crisis. Take time alone or together and write down the Bible verses that you feel apply to your situation. Don't make my mistake! Quickly invite the Lord into every crisis.

CHAPTER 9

Anger Is One Letter Away from Danger

Thought Starter

Is being a little bit angry
like being a little bit pregnant?

♦

Put off . . . anger, wrath, malice.
COLOSSIANS 3:8

Facing Anger Honestly

It is not very often that an author describes a session with his counselor. Jay Carty did just that, and I happened to be the counselor.

I was on my way to teach a class at a Christian college when I was given a note requesting that I return a long distance phone call from Jay. I returned his call and he wanted to set up an appointment. We agreed on 2:00 P.M. that day, and I hurried on to teach my class. In my rush to get to class on time, I did not make any notation about the appointment.

After class, a student invited me to play racquetball at 1:30 P.M. Our play was interrupted by a phone call: Jay Carty wanted to know why I hadn't kept my appointment.

I showered and dressed as quickly as possible, but I was still about an hour late. On the way to the appointment I breathed a prayer to the Lord to help me handle a very embarrassing situation. I walked into the room where a very understandably irate Jay Carty, six feet, seven inches tall, former professional basketball player and all muscle, was waiting with his wife. To say the least, there was a very awkward beginning. I mumbled an apology and tried to explain that I had taken the call on my way to a class and had failed to write the time in my schedule.

Jay handed me a folder containing his Taylor/Johnson Temperament Test. I could feel him glaring at me as I studied it and realized that he could be very intimidating to most people when he was angry. The test showed an extremely dominant, very hostile, strongly expressive person. I decided to take a highly aggressive approach. After all, he must have some biblical insights since he had been a camp director in a Christian camp and was now considering moving on to serve in another Christian organization.

Here is Jay's version of the meeting:

I had been directing a Christian conference center in the mountains of southern California around Lake Arrowhead. The big problems at the camp had been solved, and I knew I wasn't a fine tuner organizationally. The camp needed a true manager for the next step in its history.

I had two job options, but I couldn't decide between them. I was either going with "Churches Alive," a church disciplining organization, as their Northwest Director, or I was going to be the Team Director for Athletes in Action basketball, a ministry of Campus Crusade for Christ.

I kept vacillating. My kids were saying, "What kind of a day is it, Dad, a Churches Alive day or an A.I.A. day?" Sometimes my indecision varied hourly.

I just couldn't make up my mind; it was really tough. So we went to see Dr. Henry Brandt, a nationally acclaimed Christian counselor, and now teaching at a Christian college. I needed help, and I hoped he could give it.

San Diego is a three-hour drive from Lake Arrowhead. When Mary and I arrived, Dr. Brandt wasn't there. He had forgotten the meeting and showed up a half-hour late. I was a bit upset about waiting after such a long drive.

We took our Taylor/Johnson Temperament Analysis Tests with us. When we went into the office, the good doctor spread out the tests, looked at them, and asked "What's the problem?"

I said, "I'm having trouble making a job change and thought you could help us sort out the decision-making process."

"Well, it's easy for me to see what the problem is, Jay," Henry responded. "There's sin in your life."

After a lengthy pause I offered a rather impatient response, "Henry, perhaps you could elaborate just a little bit."

Dr. Brandt spent the next three or four minutes undressing me emotionally. I was sitting there naked in front of him; he could see who I really was, and I knew it. I was upset. Now you probably wouldn't have known I was mad. My wife knew. Henry knew because he's a pro.

So I'm sitting there mad, and Henry asks, "What seems to be bothering you, Jay?"

"Nothing!"

"Don't compound the problem by lying about it, tell me what's on your mind."

Well, he picked the right guy. My Taylor/ Johnson scored me ninety-nine percent dominant, ninety-six percent hostile, strongly expressive, and placed me considerably more subjective than objective. In other words, I'm a walking time bomb. Apart from the Holy Spirit, I'm dangerous.

"You hotshot." I was indignant. "You don't care about me, or you wouldn't have forgotten the appointment. Then you pull this grandstand move by telling me there's sin in my life, pat me on the rear, send me on my way and tell me, 'Hey, you just talked to the great Dr. Henry Brandt.' Well, thank you, but I'm not impressed. I think you're a fraud, and I think you stink."

He disarmed me with a totally emotionless question, "What else seems to be bothering you, Jay?"

There wasn't much fight left in me by this time. It's so hard to fight with someone who won't fight. I said, "Henry, never mind. Just forget about the whole thing." I motioned to Mary for us to leave.

Henry said, "No, no, don't go. Right now, how do you feel down in the pit of your stomach? Would you say the fruit of the Spirit, as defined in Galatians 5:22 and 23, typifies the way you feel: "love, joy, peace, patience, kindness, goodness, faithfulness, gentleness, and self-control?"

"That answer's easy," I snorted. "None of those qualities typify the way I feel, at least not right now."

He asked, "Then it's safe to conclude you are not filled with the Spirit of God?"

That question means lots of different things to lots of different people. Some people are really asking if you speak in tongues, but that wasn't what Henry was asking. Some people would be asking if you truly know Jesus as Savior. That wasn't what Henry was asking either. He wanted to know if I was currently experiencing the power of God in my life.

I put on my sarcastically theological facade and replied, "Now, Henry, I know Jesus Christ as Savior. My body is the dwelling place of the Holy Spirit. The Holy Spirit's in there. I've been sealed with the Holy Spirit of promise, I've been baptized into one body, and I drink of the same Spirit you do. But if what you're talking about is the essence of Ephesians 5:18 (being constantly in the process of being filled or empowered by the Holy Spirit), then I'm not filled. Oh, it's true, the Spirit's in here," as I pointed to my body, "but right now He doesn't have all of me. I'm mad, and I've spent some time dwelling on my anger. As I understand it, until he has one hundred percent of me, I'm not filled. If that's what you're talking about, then I'm not filled because none of the qualities you just mentioned are currently evident in my life."

"That's right," he said. "If the qualities aren't there, you can't be filled." He asked again, "You're sure you're not filled?"

"I'm sure," I growled. "Right now I'm not filled, I'm real mad. I mean, I'm really mad at you, and I'm not handling it well. Henry, you may not know it, but your upper lip is in danger of being pulled up over your forehead."

Remember, I ran a Christian camp, and in Christian camping you live on the grounds, and everybody with whom you work lives on the grounds. In other words, you live with the same people you work with. You can't get away from each other, except by going into your living quarters. So when you get one or two fellow workers who irritate you, you're irritated most of the time. That was me for sure.

It was then he asked me the blockbuster question. He asked gently, in a soft voice that was such a contrast to mine, "Jay, do you feel that way most of the time?"

It was so quiet you could hear our breathing. "Yes."

It was true. Anger was an ongoing problem for me. I guess it started early in my life. Anger is often a problem for people who have had an alcoholic parent and who went through their parent's divorce during early teenage years. I had quit a good job, an executive position. We sold a wonderful home in Corona del Mar in the Newport Beach area of southern California, with a view of the sun setting behind Catalina Island every night. We had keys to a private beach. I worked four minutes from my house and actually went home for lunch each day. Talk about having it made! We did, but we flicked it all in to go serve God. Then, four and a half years later, I discovered I'd been serving Him in the power of my flesh, not in the power of the Spirit. You see, I was mad most of the time.

I said, "Henry, how bad am I? What am I going to do? I've only spent a lifetime learning to live this way."

"It's like having a splinter in your thumb," Henry responded. "You hurt your thumb a lot because you use it a lot. But if you pull the splinter, the thumb gets well rather quickly."

"Please tell me how."

"Confess it to God."

I was still puzzled. "What are you talking about? How?" I was pleading now.

"Whenever you feel anger, talk to God about it before you sin. You might have to do it twenty times the first day, but it will only require eighteen the second. As you practice, your confession frequency will continue to decrease. You might go a few days or even a week or so without having to do it."[1]

Jay Carty was a man who had wrestled most of his life with anger. He experienced a miracle with his anger. I didn't solve his anger problem; God did. Today, he is an easy going, cheerful, gentle person. What made the difference? He got hold of the simple truth that Jesus died to save us from our sins and make His Spirit available to us. He trained himself to be alert to the first signs of anger, turn at once to God for cleansing, and to be empowered by God's Holy Spirit. Today, Jay has an ever-widening speaking ministry in which he teaches people how to yield themselves to God's control.

During my meeting with Jay and his wife, I did not go into his past feelings toward his father or his mother or how his parents' divorce affected him when he was younger. Our discussion lasted twenty to thirty minutes and focused on his sinful behavior of anger. I just directed him to the healing power of God in order to deal with the sin in his life today. God may have later brought issues from his past to his mind that needed attention, but the immediate issue was his current anger. This is the miracle available to everyone: we are a prayer away from peace and freedom from anger.

How fast can someone become angry? Five seconds is not too fast, is it? If I can get angry in less than five seconds, I can get un-angry in the time it takes to breathe a simple prayer. It *is* just that simple! It has worked in my own life and in thousands of lives over the years.

It is also true that I don't understand the complete situation in people's lives. And neither do you or any other counselor. But God does. That's why we bring our anger to Him: He understands us and loves us and wants us to be free from anger.

The Consuming Nature of Anger

Some people relish and enjoy their anger. Frederick Buechner says it clearly:

> Of the Seven Deadly Sins, anger is possibly the most fun. To lick your wounds, to smack your lips over grievances long past, to roll over your tongue the prospect of bitter confrontations still to come, to savor to the last toothsome morsel both the pain you are given and the pain you are giving back; in many ways it is a feast fit for a king. The chief drawback is that what you are wolfing down is yourself. *The skeleton at the feast is you.*[2]

Anger is the universal problem. I have never met anyone, anywhere in the world, who has escaped the destructive force of anger, or who has never experienced someone else's anger as a destructive force.

Some writers say anger is neither good nor bad. It all depends on how you use it. Some writers use the term "righteous indignation" which motivates a person to correct mistreatment and injustices; if this is correct, then people will be angry the rest of their lives because there is always something you can be angry about. Some go so far as to say that anger is God-given.

The Latin root for anger is *angere* which means "to strangle." I find that the definition of anger helps clarify the real situation: "Anger: emotional reaction, of displeasure and/or antagonism; an impulse to retaliate, punish, seek revenge. Anger can vary in intensity from mild annoyance that is hardly noticeable to extreme overmastering rage resembling insanity. Anger can trigger an outward display ranging from a light change of expression to destruction or murder; from a mild word to enraged screaming."

Personally, I have never experienced anger within my body as a positive force. It has *always* been a hindrance to intelligent, straight thinking and constructive, rational behavior. In my work as a counselor and business consultant, I have never observed anger to be a positive factor in problem solving. I have never found anger to be righteous. From the slightest shade of anger that we may not even be conscious of to the anger that leads to murder, it is all cut from the same cloth.

In an instant, anger can change a person from being satisfied, cheerful, and relaxed to being dissatisfied, unhappy, and tense. Oddly enough, this sudden change within the body is triggered by something that happens outside the body. Life would be much more pleasant, comfortable, and relaxing if only we could find its cause and cure.

If there is a topic about which there is universal agreement, it would be this: *unrestrained anger can destroy us.* It cannot be ignored. It must be tamed.

But if there is a topic about which there is universal disagreement, it would be how to tame anger.

If there is anger in your heart, someone may either do or not do something that instantly triggers anger inside of you. Someone may say or not say something that immediately triggers your anger. Something happens or fails to happen that triggers your anger. Thoughts about the past, present, or future can trigger your anger. Angry emotions "can vary in intensity from mild annoyance that is hardly noticeable to extreme overmastering rage that resembles insanity."

The Physical Aspects of Anger

Anger produces disagreeable bodily changes that cannot be ignored. Almost everyone is familiar with the following:

+ heart beats faster
+ blood pressure rises
+ the throat tightens
+ mouth is dry
+ gooseflesh appears
+ hair is erect
+ pupils of the eyes open wide
+ eyeballs glisten
+ person sweats, blushes, turns pale
+ muscles tense
+ highly alert
+ desire for physical action increases
+ insomnia may be present
+ problems with the colon and/or stomach problems appear

Anger can trigger some action ranging from just a slight change of expression to destruction or murder. Anger may result in a mild word or enraged screaming. Anger can, but seldom does, motivate a person to seek changes that will improve the environment that triggers the anger.

To grasp how frustrating anger can be, look at the range of people who can trigger an anger response in you: babies, parents, marriage partners, children, friends, people at work, total strangers, yourself, clerks, neighbors, officials, people in social gatherings.

Circumstances can also trigger anger. The range varies greatly. P. T. Young reports the results of asking a group of college students to keep records of what stimulated them to an angry reaction. Here are the results: unjust accusations, insulting remarks, not being invited to a party, disobedience of children, criticisms, contradictions, scoldings, unwelcome advice, work left undone, being locked out, money being lost, sleep interrupted, physical pain, thwarting self-expression.[3]

Recently, someone even told me that he was angry at the weather. I am sure that you can also add to the above list.

The question is: "Can God help?" The answer is emphatically, "Yes!" His help is decidedly different from human or self-help.

The Biblical View of Anger

Many people who know very little about Jesus do know that He threw the moneychangers out of the temple. See Matthew 21:12–15; Mark 11:15–18; and Luke 19:45–47.

Others who know very little about the Bible know about another verse:

"In your anger do not sin:
Do not let the sun go down
while you are still angry."
EPHESIANS 4:26, NIV

People use these few verses to justify their anger. I take this verse to mean that if you are aware of being angry you should deal with it quickly. The deadline is sundown.

Anger is a normal response to unrighteousness. Can we conclude then, that our anger is God-given and alerts and energizes us into action to see that wrongs are made right? Or should we conclude that "normal responses" are not necessarily "Godly responses."

As I study the Bible, I do not find that we are instructed to vent our anger against evil causes or toward evil people. Evaluate these verses:

"Love your enemies,
bless those who curse you,
do good to those who hate you,
and pray for those who spitefully use you
and persecute you . . .
[The Father] makes His sun rise
on the evil and on the good."
MATTHEW 5:44–45

Husbands, love your wives
just as Christ also loved the church and
gave Himself for her.
EPHESIANS 5:25

That they admonish the young women
to love their husbands, to love their children.
TITUS 2:4

"'You shall love your neighbor as yourself.'"
MATTHEW 22:39

Beloved, do not avenge yourselves,
but rather give place to wrath;
for it is written,
"Vengeance is Mine, I will repay,"
says the Lord.

ROM. 12:19

Love the brotherhood.

1 PETER 2:17

Abound in love to one another and to all.

1 THESSALONIANS 3:12

If we eliminate all of the above people as objects of our anger, who is left to be the object of our anger?

The Bible does state that anger is a natural expression of our humanness; it is a natural expression of our "old man" and "the old sin nature." But the Bible says that anger is "sin" and it is not OK.

Look at what the Bible says about man's anger:

The wrath of man does not produce
the righteousness of God.

JAMES 1:20

Cease from anger,
and forsake wrath;
do not fret—it only causes harm.

PSALMS 37:8

Do not hasten in your spirit to be angry,
for anger rests in the bosom of fools.

ECCLESIASTES 7:9

Make no friendship with an angry man,
and with a furious man do not go,
lest you learn his ways and
set a snare for your soul.

PROVERBS 22:24–25

He who is a quick-tempered man acts foolishly.

PROVERBS 14:17

He who is slow to anger is better than the mighty,
and he who rules his spirit than he who takes a city.

PROVERBS 16:32

"Whoever is angry with his brother without a cause
shall be in danger of the judgment."

MATTHEW 5:22

Let all bitterness, wrath, anger, clamor,
and evil speaking be put away from you,
with all malice.

EPHESIANS 4:31

Put off all these: anger, wrath, malice.

COLOSSIANS 3:8

[Lay] aside all malice.

1 PETER 2:1

Anger is a universal fact of life. Law enforcement people report that at least half of the homicides committed in this country involve people who know each other. Millions of women are beaten up each year by their husbands. Millions of children are abused each year by angry parents. At any time it seems that people experience an explosion of varying degrees of intensity of displeasure, antagonism, belligerence, rage, and violent passion.

The difficult problem is how can a human being who naturally responds angrily to the circumstances of life change from responding in anger to responding in love? Humanly speaking, we must admit that this biblical advice is impossible to attain. We all know that to bottle up or swallow your anger is no solution. Bottled-up anger can ruin your health, twist your thinking, and make you a walking time bomb, set to explode at some external provocation. What can a person do? You can attempt to manage this anger yourself or you can turn to God for help. Humanly speaking, what can you do to tame your anger?

Many children are victims of anger expression. Some advice was proposed in a newspaper advertisement by the National Committee for Prevention of Child Abuse. It was entitled *12 Alternatives To Whacking Your Kid.* The ad advised that when big and little problems of your everyday life pile up to the point where you feel like lashing out, stop! Take time out. Don't take it out on your kid. Try any or all of these simple alternatives—whatever works for you. The ad goes on to list twelve:

1. Stop in your tracks. Step back. Sit down.
2. Take five deep breaths. Inhale. Exhale, slowly, slowly.
3. Count to ten. Better yet, twenty. Or say the alphabet out loud.
4. Phone a friend. A relative. Even the weather.
5. Still mad? Punch a pillow. Or munch an apple.
6. Thumb through a magazine, book, newspaper, photo album.

7. Do some sit-ups.
8. Pick up a pencil and write down your thoughts.
9. Take a hot bath, or a cold shower.
10. Lie down on the floor, or just put your feet up.
11. Put on your favorite record.
12. Water your plants.

I was reading an article on anger management while traveling in an airplane. This is typical advice offered by anger management professionals. The authors proposed four steps:

1. *Cool off before you sound off.* They made suggestions similar to the newspaper ad.

2. *Identify what causes you to feel anger.* How do you take criticism or teasing? Develop an awareness of what triggers your anger.

3. *How can you make anger work for you?* Learn what forms of anger expression are acceptable to your colleagues. Find something constructive that you can do to work off your anger.

4. Communicate your anger. Use facts and objective information that others need to know about you. Help them see that your response was appropriate and reasonable. Develop information so you can help each other avoid anger-producing situations.[4]

Is it really true that we must live with angry responses all our lives? Is there no other way to find freedom from anger than in perfecting self-control, resolving human-relation problems, and altering the circumstances we get plunged into? Is there no other way than to back off and calm down?

As far as I know, that's all anyone humanly speaking knows to do at this point in history. This is the struggle that the humanist must live with because anger happens so fast you often act before you know it.

The Bible offers a radical solution: "Put it away. Stop it." This is humanly impossible. Yes, it takes a miracle. You need supernatural help.

Dealing with Anger Biblically

There are two basic steps in dealing with anger from a biblical perspective.

Step #1: Recognize Anger As Sin.

God's prescription for dealing with destructive anger is precise and strong. Strife, malice, hatred, anger, outbursts of wrath, dissension, and contention are works of the flesh which are of the sinful nature. (Gal. 5:19–21)

Anger is sin, and that's good news! There is a divine solution for sin. God promised to help you. Dealing with sin is His specialty.

> [Jesus] will save His people from their sins.
> MATTHEW 1:21

> Nor is there salvation in any other,
> for there is no other name under heaven
> given among men by which we must be saved.
> ACTS 4:12

A simple step that gives you the strength to "stop" angry

responses is to invite Jesus to come into your life. Competent, able people have a hard time accepting the fact that we need supernatural help. "I can manage my anger. Isn't that good enough?" It certainly beats exploding. The best you can do is to manage your anger. Only God can help you to "stop" because *anger is sin.* Therefore, humans need a Savior who will cleanse us of our sins.

It is not inevitable that we must spend the rest of our lives struggling with anger. Anger can be "put away." Once we accept the fact that anger is sin and we need a Savior, we can practice a simple biblical directive daily if necessary:

> **If we confess our sins,**
> **He is faithful and just to forgive us our sins**
> **and to cleanse us from all unrighteousness.**
> 1 JOHN 1:9

He will cleanse the anger out of our hearts. Anger is not good. Anger interferes with my thinking process. It is bad. It is destructive. It is sin.

Step #2: Replace Anger with the Fruit of the Spirit.
When you have a forgiven, cleansed heart, you can ask God for the power of the Holy Spirit to produce the fruit of the Spirit in your life:

> **Love, joy, peace, longsuffering, kindness, goodness,**
> **faithfulness, gentleness, self-control.**
> GALATIANS 5:22–23

You will still have problems. You will face injustices and difficult people, just as everyone else does. You will still need to be energized, alerted, and motivated to correct what needs correcting. But God knows that a person energized by the Holy Spirit with love, joy, peace, longsuffering, kindness, goodness, faithfulness, gentleness and self-control has the strength to conquer bitterness, sarcastic words, anxiety, bodily tensions, or violent behavior that formerly characterized him.

The apostle Paul says it best:

> "Walk in the Spirit
> and you shall not fulfill the lust of the flesh."
> GALATIANS 5:16

A Christian does not always surrender to God perfectly, anymore than he can manage himself perfectly. Few people make it through any given day perfectly. But you can catch anger at the earliest possible point. When you realize you have sinned, take it to God.

As the apostle John says:

> My little children,
> these things I write to you,
> so that you may not sin.
> And if anyone sins,
> we have an Advocate with the Father,
> Jesus Christ the righteous.
> And He Himself is the propitiation
> [the one who paid our debt with His life]
> for our sins,
> and not for ours only
> but also for the whole world.
> 1 JOHN 2:1–2

CHAPTER 10

Your Wife has Inoperable Cancer

Thought Starter

Is the peace of God that guards your heart and mind available in a crisis?

Be anxious for nothing,
but in everything by prayer and supplication,
with thanksgiving,
let your requests be made known to God;
and the peace of God,
which surpasses all understanding,
will guard your hearts and minds
through Christ Jesus.

PHILIPPIANS 4:6–7

God's Peace Is Beyond Our Human Understanding

It had been about two years since Eva had her operation. Her cancer problem was behind her, and we had planned to spend Thanksgiving with our daughter Beth and her family. Instead, Eva was in a hospital in Florida. Shortly after Eva had been wheeled into the operating room, the surgeon came to us with the chilling and terrifying news that she had inoperable cancer and had six months to a year to live.

At first, the news left us stunned! Surely, we thought, there must be a way to overcome this problem. The doctors proposed a combination of chemical and radiation therapy. Eva and I didn't sleep well for several nights as we absorbed the reality of this news.

We were forced to take an in-depth look at just what peace is. We had spent the previous thirty-five years studying and searching for correct principles to live by. Most of what we had found was from the Bible, and we had traveled the world trying to teach what we had learned. Over the years, the most common problem we had seen was people who were struggling in their quest for peace. Now we were being given one of life's acid tests: Can you have peace during a painful death?

Where Does Peace Come From?

Together my wife and I found several verses that directed us to the God of peace:

Now may the Lord of peace Himself
give you peace always in every way.
The Lord be with you all.
2 THESSALONIANS 3:16

Be anxious for nothing,
but in everything by prayer and supplication,
with thanksgiving,
let your requests be made known to God;
and the peace of God,
which surpasses all understanding,
will guard your hearts and minds
through Christ Jesus.
PHILIPPIANS 4:6–7

These things I have spoken to you,
that in Me you may have peace.
In the world you will have tribulation;
but be of good cheer,
I have overcome the world.
JOHN 16:33

Let the peace of God rule in your hearts
. . . and be thankful.
COLOSSIANS 3:15

These verses made it clear that peace is something that originates with God and is available to us under any conditions which included our present circumstances. Philippians 4:6–7 indicated clearly that God's peace is beyond our human understanding. Even though it is real and I have experienced it over the years, I still don't understand it and can't really explain it. It just works.

Picture a peaceful person with relaxed muscles, normal blood pressure, a quiet mind, and a calm and contented heart. Consider the opposite: tense, anxious, stressful, and uneasy. We had to face the fact that we were not peaceful.

How can you be peaceful when you face a painful, slow death? How can you be peaceful when you have tough decisions to make? For example, what do you do about a specialist's recommendation that you undergo chemical and radiation therapy and when another specialist doesn't recommend it? When you pray and ask God for guidance and there is only silence? When you receive solicited and unsolicited conflicting advice from many friends and associates who care deeply?

We turned to our Guidebook for help. These were the time-proven instructions that we already knew, and they needed to be applied to our new circumstances. Never before had we faced a situation like this one.

> Trust in the LORD with all your heart,
> and lean not on your own understanding.
> In all your ways acknowledge Him,
> and He shall direct your paths.
> PROVERBS 3:5–6

If you combine this verse with Philippians 4:6–7 and John 16:33, it is clear that if you want to get a hearing from God you need to present your "requests" to Him in a relaxed, cheerful, thankful, trusting fashion. We may have an opinion about how things should turn out, but we need to be neutral about how they actually do turn out.

The Anxiety of a Crisis

Eva and I had very definite opinions about how this situation should turn out. She had always been a healthy woman. We wanted her to be healed! Why should a good woman who has been faithful to God, her husband, and her family suffer a slow, painful death by cancer? It didn't make sense. Of course we were anxious! Why shouldn't we be?

But the Bible said we needed to come to the Lord in the proper spirit. The Bible said to relax and trust God. We asked the Lord to help us, and we experienced a miracle. He did calm us down, and we were able to trust Him.

Eva decided that she didn't want the chemical and radiation therapy. Our research indicated that this might prolong her life a bit, but only at the cost of intense suffering. She preferred to try a special diet and food supplement program.

When we let a specialist and some of our friends know about our decision, we experienced a chorus of intensive opposition. I was confronted by some of our best friends who said we must avail ourselves of the finest medical technique available. They insisted I would never be able to forgive myself if I didn't do this.

When the judgment of people we respected was so strong against our decision, Eva and I had to reconsider. We prayed fervently for direction. Silence.

I remembered a time when Moses was in need of direction. He cried out to the Lord, and the Lord gave him this answer:

> "My presence will go with you,
> and I will give you rest."
>
> EXODUS 33:14

163

That seemed to be our answer. Eva did not change her mind, and we proceeded with our plan. We discovered that we could not commit our ways unto Him once and for all. We found ourselves drifting away again and again from peaceful trust in God.

Eva could not follow the rigorous diet and food supplement program that she had selected. Slowly she lost weight: 120 pounds, 110 pounds, 100 pounds, 90 pounds. Sincerely concerned people came to call on us. They asked about our faith. A prayer of faith should heal her. We were asked if there was any known sin in our lives. We appreciated their interest. We searched our hearts and as best we could tell, there was nothing that blocked our prayers for healing.

Several dear people proposed that our faith was too weak. They would pray for Eva themselves and we could benefit from their faith.

Eva just lost more weight and got weaker and weaker. She stuck to her decision not to have chemical therapy. Weeks grew into months as we observed a steady physical decline. At the same time, our faith and trust in the Lord grew. We realized that peace was not dependent on God's doing what we wanted Him to do, but peace was dependent on knowing that He was God and that He knew what was best in every situation.

Our daughter Sue was able to spend the last six months of Eva's life with her. She was a missionary with the North American Indian Mission with which we had worked since she was a teenager. Now that Eva was sick, the mission assigned her to look after her mother. I canceled most of my itinerary and also spent the last six months of her life with her. Numerous other people spent several days to a week helping to keep the home going. Our whole family gathered together for Christmas. Mel and Bertha Willett spent five or six weeks near the end of Eva's life. Tom and Ruth Tate, dear friends for thirty years, took a week out of a very busy life to be with Eva. We were surrounded by many people from all over the world; they offered sympathy, friendship, and help with housekeeping, cooking, and running errands.

Trusting God in All Circumstances

Notwithstanding the prayers of people all over the world, Eva continued to fail. One day it hit me more clearly than ever that she would die. It made me mad, and I let God know it! Like many people in my situation, I had refused to accept the obvious. One day as I was leaving our condominium, walking toward the elevator and venting my wrath at God, a presence seemed to be in that hallway. It was as if a voice spoke: "Trust me. I am God. Let Me comfort you and give you peace. I will not change Eva's condition. You want to be angry and rebellious about it. I want you to let Me change your heart."

Once more, I needed to return to trusting God. I needed to repent and let Him calm me down again, and again commit Eva into His loving care.

About six weeks before she died, Eva told me the pain was becoming more intense. She became so preoccupied with her pain that she couldn't think about anything else. She asked me to keep reminding her to look to God for peace. When she was relaxed, she said, the pain was less.

We prayed for wisdom. About that time, Dr. Steiner from Buffalo dropped in to see us. He taught us some relaxation techniques that helped greatly to relieve her pain. Together, Eva and I asked the Lord to teach us how to help her to be peaceful. We created a plan that combined physical relaxation and yielding her heart to the Lord.

For physical relaxation we did what Dr. Steiner taught us. I would kneel beside the bed and whisper to Eva, "Tighten your toe muscles and let them go. Tighten your foot muscles and let them go. Tighten your ankle muscles and let them go. Tighten your calf muscles and let them go." We worked this way with all the muscles from the bottom of her feet to the top of her head. I will be eternally grateful to Dr. Steiner for his help.

In addition, we chose some Scripture verses that I repeated after the physical relaxation exercises. I would whisper:

> This is the day which the LORD has made;
> we will rejoice and be glad in it.
> PSALMS 118:24

> For this day is holy to our LORD.
> Do not sorrow,
> for the joy of the LORD
> is your strength.
> NEHEMIAH 8:10

> Let the peace of God rule in your hearts
> . . . and be thankful.
> COLOSSIANS 3:15

Then I would whisper, "Let the Lord give you peace. Just let Him give you joy. You need more today than you ever needed in your whole life." By the time we finished this, she had drifted away into blessed, peaceful sleep.

We repeated this routine six, eight, ten times in a day. Sometimes she would call me; sometimes on my own I felt the urge to go to her. We looked forward to these little meetings, and we actually "enjoyed" them in that we both knew we were participants in something beyond human understanding.

I do not for a moment discount the wonderful support, affection, sympathy, and help given to us by beloved friends. We had the best that human beings can give. However, we all witnessed something supernatural happening to Eva in those last several weeks of her life.

She continued to lose weight until she was down to seventy pounds. She became more and more serene as the end neared. There was a kind of angelic aura of joyful peace about her.

She allowed the peace of God that surpasses understanding to guard her heart and mind through Jesus Christ. This was Eva's final word by living it out in her life:

> And the peace of God,
> which surpasses all understanding,
> will guard your hearts and minds.
> PHILIPPIANS 4:7

Living and Dying

> It is appointed for men to die once,
> but after this the judgment.
> HEBREWS 9:27

> For what is a man profited
> if he gains the whole world,
> and loses his own soul?
> MATTHEW 16:26

It was April 25, 1982. Eva and I were alone in her private hospital room as she battled cancer. She was lying in bed with her head propped up on pillows when I heard her weak little voice say, "Am I going to die?"

I was stunned and not prepared for her question. I have always been forthright with Eva, but I was greatly tempted to lie to her. After a long pause, I heard myself say, "Yes, you are going to die."

She said, "I'm scared."

I asked, "Why are you scared?"

She said, "Because I made a mess of my life."

How could she say such a thing? This lady who had traveled the world by my side, who was my stable companion, who kept encouraging me, who left a heritage to a host of women whom she helped to understand their role as wife and mother, and who was a faithful career mother?

I asked, "Why do you say this?"

Her answer was a complete surprise. "I could have been a better mother. I could have been more careful with the money. I could have been a better witness. I could have been more affectionate toward you."

How should I respond? I was always proud of the way she handled her role as a mother. It's true, she could have been more careful with money, but what did it matter now? There are very few women who served the Lord as she did. As far as being more affectionate toward me, only she would know.

My first impulse was to reassure her that she was wrong. But then I remembered many instances when, after listening to someone unburden themselves to us, we were tempted to soft-pedal their story. The only way to really help them was not to offer human sympathy but to help them call sin by its right name.

These thoughts ran through my mind. Eva was about to meet Jesus. She wasn't concerned about her plants or her wardrobe or her makeup. She was concerned about her soul.

Prepared for the Journey

Finally I whispered, "You know what we would advise people who told us a story like that, don't you?"
She answered:

> **"If you will confess your sins,**
> **He is faithful and just**
> **to forgive us our sins**
> **and to cleanse us**
> **from all unrighteousness."**
> 1 JOHN 1:9

She went on to tell the Lord what she told me. I could hardly hear her voice. As she prayed, it dawned on me that everything she said was true of me. I could have been a better father, more careful with the money, a better witness, more affectionate toward Eva.

When Eva finished her prayer, I prayed my prayer. Two weary pilgrims in a hospital room, getting our hearts cleaned up by the living God. I look back on that incident as one of the most inspiring, refreshing, renewing moments in our forty-two years of marriage. It was a final tune-up before the supreme event of all: preparing to meet the Lord.

The next day I was alone with Eva in her room. She was alert and seemed supernaturally peaceful.

I asked, "Are you scared today?"
She said, "No, not at all."
I asked, "Why not?"
She said, with a broad smile, "I got the garbage cleaned out of my heart last night."
I asked, "Are you ready to go?"
"Yes," she said.

Some visitors dropped in. When they left, I asked her if she would like to talk to our daughter Beth because our son Dick and his wife, Patti, had called the day before. I dialed the number and Eva chatted with Beth.

About a half hour later, Eva dozed off. I noticed that she was breathing unusually heavy. Just then, Sue, our daughter who was helping me take care of Eva, walked in. Together we watched Eva take a final breath and she was gone. I heard Sue say, "Praise the Lord." I agreed. What a wonderful experience. She was with the Lord whom we loved and served.

> Precious in the sight of the LORD
> is the death of His saints
>
> PSALMS 116:15

I cannot and could not look at her death as a tragedy. I suppose it all depends on your preparation. We really believe that to meet Jesus is the ultimate, supreme event of life.

Recently, I talked to a couple who had not seen their son for four years because he was in another country getting an education. Of course they missed him, but they would not for one moment deprive him of that privilege.

I look at Eva's death in the same way. What a privilege for her to go on ahead to meet Jesus. Of course we miss her, but we would not for one moment deprive her of that privilege.

There were piles of cards that arrived after Eva died. One stood out that came from Dr. Earl Radmacher, the president of Western Baptist Seminary:

"The Ship"

I am standing upon the seashore. A ship at my side spreads her sails to the morning breeze and starts for the blue ocean. She is an object of beauty and strength and I watch her until at length she hangs like a speck of white cloud just where the sea and sky come down to mingle with each other. Then someone at my side says, "There, she's gone."

"Gone where?" Gone from my sight . . . that is all. She is as large in mast and hull and spar as she was when she left my side, and just as able to bear her load of living freight to the place of destination. Her diminished size is in me, not in her; and just at that moment when someone at my side says, "there she's gone," there are other voices ready to take up the glad shout, "Here she comes!"

And that is dying.[1]

> "Come, you blessed of My Father,
> inherit the kingdom prepared for you
> from the foundation of the world."
> MATTHEW 25:34

The key to anticipating the death of the people we know and love is *preparation*. When you love someone as much as you do the Lord and He calls that person to come to Him, you will be pleased with His decision. This is the ultimate, crowning event that all of us will experience if we meet the conditions. A warm welcome from the One who loves us is what we eagerly anticipate if our conscience is clear.

I later found a note among Eva's papers, dated January 10, 1982:

Through this experience I've had the joy and comfort of having my family and friends upholding me in prayer and supporting me in every way. This has given strength, relaxation, and a deep sense of comfort and peace; and to know God has been with me, near me, beside me, with the promise: "I will *never* leave thee nor forsake thee," what perfect peace and comfort this has been! Jesus had to suffer that awful experience of separation from *His Father,* He suffered alone, I have never experienced this!

She died April 26, 1982.

> O Death, where is your sting?
> O Hades, where is your victory?
> 1 CORINTHIANS 15:55

Prepared for this World

Are most of us too busy to hear God's whispers; does it take a clap of thunder to get our attention?

> "For what is a man profited
> if he gains the whole world,
> and loses his own soul?"
> MATTHEW 16:26

Watching events unfold in my life and noting my responses to them have helped me draw some personal conclusions about this world.

Conclusion #1: Loving God Means Obeying God

> "'You shall love the LORD your God
> with all your heart,
> with all your soul,
> and with all your mind.'"
> MATTHEW 22:37

This command was a puzzle to me for a long time. How can I tell how much I love God? Is loving God in conflict with loving my family? Then one day I received a very clear answer given by Jesus himself:

**He who has My commandments
and keeps them,
it is he who loves Me.**
JOHN 14:21

If I love Him, I will study and *obey* His commandments as the single top priority of my life. Observing whether I am obeying Him is a quick check to see if I have a rebellious spirit. He said that to love God is the greatest commandment of them all.

Conclusion #2: Loving God Means Loving Your Neighbor

"'You shall love your neighbor as yourself.'"
MATTHEW 22:39

Jesus said that this is the second greatest commandment of them all and it is like the first. This commandment has two sides to it. Jesus said that I am to look after my own soul as a priority equal to loving God:

**"For what is a man profited
if he gains the whole world,
and loses his own soul."**
MATTHEW 16:26

The other side of the command is to love everyone and be as concerned about their souls as my own.

Conclusion #3: Loving God Means Being a Steward

The earth is the LORD's.
PSALMS 24:1

This fact has been a source of great freedom to me. I don't own anything. I am a steward of someone else's property. It belongs to the One I am to love with all my heart, soul, and mind. If I do, then I will care for His property as if it were my own. The Bible tells me that all that is in the world will be burned up. If that is true, then I need to heed the advice of my friend, Jack Klemke: to hold the things in the world lightly. It will all become an ash pile. Only people will be left!

Conclusion #4: Loving God Means Wanting to Meet Him

It is appointed for men to die once,
but after this the judgment.
HEBREWS 9:27

This ought to be welcome, exciting news. Recently my wife, Jo, and I went to visit her ninety-nine-year-old mother-in-law. Jo eagerly looked forward to this visit. The closer we got, the more excited she got. Finally, Jo saw her: the crowning moment of a long journey to Salem, Oregon. What a pleasure to greet someone whom you love! Who would want to withhold such a privilege from anyone?

After meeting the Lord comes the judgment. If I have kept His commandments (the test of our love), then I can anticipate this greeting:

"'Come, you blessed of My Father,
inherit the kingdom prepared for you

from the foundation of the world.'"
MATTHEW 25:34)

Happy thought!

Conclusion #5: Loving God Prepares Us to Lose Our Christian Friends

> Precious in the sight of the LORD
> is the death of His saints.
> PSALMS 116:15

The key to anticipating the death of the people I know and love is *preparation*. When I love someone as much as I love the Lord and He calls that person to come to Him, I will be pleased with His decision, provided my conscience is clear toward that person. This is the crowning event for the people we love: a warm welcome from our Lord.

Conclusion #6: Loving God Involves Growing in Grace and Knowledge

> Grow in the grace and knowledge
> of our Lord and Savior Jesus Christ.
> To Him be the glory
> both now and forever.
> 2 PETER 3:18

Preparation for meeting the God I care about is a happy task. As I prepare and wait, I remember these things:

♦ Grow in grace. The ultimate achievement in yielding to the grace of God is to become more gracious as I grow older.

- Grow in the knowledge of the Lord Jesus Christ. The more I study His commandments and do them, the more my appreciation of the benefits of obedience grows.
- Glorify Him: now and forever with my thoughts, emotions, and behavior. My decision to please God in these ways must be renewed day by day.

CHAPTER 11

I Prayed,
but I Still Didn't Feel Right

Thought Starter

Why do you feel good after praying sometimes,
and other times you are anxious?

◆

For the eyes of the LORD are on the righteous,
And His ears are open to their prayers;
But the face of the LORD is against those who do evil.

1 PETER 3:12

Be anxious for nothing,
but in everything by prayer and supplication,
with thanksgiving,
let your requests be made known to God;
and the peace of God,
which surpasses all understanding,
will guard your hearts and minds
through Christ Jesus.

PHILIPPIANS 4:6–7

The Need for Prayer

I was asked to speak to a group gathered for "a day of prayer." This was a good assignment because like most speakers, I usually learned more in preparation for the presentation than the audience did in listening to the message. I spent three days thumbing through my Bible, reflecting and meditating on the subject of prayer.

Looking back, I did a lot of praying while Eva was struggling with cancer and also when my second wife, Marcey, died suddenly. I did a lot of praying before Jo and I married. There have been other crises in my life when I pleaded with God to help me solve a problem. But upon reflection, I have found that it is very easy to drift away from watching God work.

A day of prayer or, more precisely, an annual day of prayer served me well. It gave me a chance to pause, to let the world go by for a day, and to contemplate the privilege of talking things over with the Creator of the universe.

The verses at the head of this chapter promises the peace that passes understanding will guard our hearts and minds as a by-product of prayer: a peace that is a quiet, still, calm, serene state of heart and mind. Everyone seeks this, but not everyone wants to meet the conditions. Prayer and supplication imply the acceptance of the truth that you must submissively and earnestly relinquish control over the events of your life to Someone else.

This proposition is a bit much for "modern" self-sufficient people who may have achieved an education, a position, wealth, power, or authority, without giving God a thought. Why should they turn control of their lives over to anyone, even God?

The answer is that sooner or later, a peaceful heart and mind will elude you. Personal attainment, competence, and intelligence are heady stuff, but not the keys to finding the peace of God. Truly self-sufficient people find this hard to believe.

I remember sitting across the desk from a businessman who had all the benefits of success: a large, beautifully decorated home located on spacious, well-tended grounds, a summer home, a farm, the finest food, clothing, cars, and the privilege of frequent travel to other countries. He achieved it on his own, yet now he was telling me how and why he needed the Lord.

He and his wife had been invited to attend an executive seminar a year earlier by several men whom he respected. On the way to the seminar, they rode in silence the whole three hours, nursing mutual hostility toward each other, in luxurious, air-conditioned comfort. They were utterly miserable; this was the third straight day they had not spoken to each other.

They sat in the audience and listened to other businessmen and their wives give their testimonies that they had achieved everything on their own except peace and contentment. Only when they turned control of their lives over to God were they able to experience the peace that passes understanding.

Separately at the conference, both he and his wife prayed and turned control of their lives over to the Lord. This simple step added the missing link for them: access to the peace of God that passes understanding.

A statement once caught my attention. I wrote it down but failed to record the source: "It would seem that a good head, excellent vision, a strong heart, a strong body, an inexhaustible purse; you'd have it made."

Not so when it comes to finding peace of heart and mind. Augustine once said to God: "You made us for Yourself, and our heart is restless until it finds rest in You."

Even Jesus, God's own Son, needed to turn His life over to the Father. When He was about to be crucified, He made a request to God:

> "Father,
> if it is Your will,
> remove this cup from Me;
> nevertheless not My will,
> but Yours, be done."
> LUKE 22:42

The answer was no. Finishing the task was necessary. It seems that everyone takes his turn in enduring something he would rather not face.

The Method of Prayer

Jesus cautioned His disciples about just giving the appearance of praying to God:

> "When you pray,
> you shall not be like the hypocrites.

For they love to pray standing in the synagogues
and on the corners of streets,
that they may be seen by men.
Assuredly, I say to you,
they have their reward."

MATTHEW 6:5–6

I am reminded of some lines in Shakespeare's *Hamlet:*

My words fly up
My thoughts remain below
Words without thoughts
Never to heaven go.[1]

I am ashamed to say it, but as I look back, I can recall instances when, as a part of an audience, I was asked to come to the platform to pray without any warning or preparation. On the way to the platform, I would pull together some random thoughts. I'd ask the audience to bow their heads to pray with me. Most of them would dutifully do so, and I'd speak some words. When finished, I could hardly remember what I had said. I doubt whether the audience did either. I'm not sure my words got beyond the ceiling.

It's a simple matter to say, "Let us pray." It is equally simple to close our eyes and bow our heads. We can join a group for "a day of prayer." All this can be done without praying. Jesus once chided the scribes and Pharisees:

"These people draw near to Me
with their mouth,
and honor Me with their lips,
but their heart is far from Me."

MATTHEW 15:8

Making our requests known to God is one kind of praying. The decision regarding our requests is His. The evidence that you have really gotten through to God is that "the peace of God that passes all understanding, will guard your heart and mind through Christ Jesus." Then, you "watch God work."

When Eva was struggling with cancer, we both requested that she be healed. We both recognized that the decision was out of our hands. Close friends urged us to exercise faith. They said that the evidence of adequate faith was her healing.

Neither Eva nor I could accept that idea. To us, the evidence of faith was peace that passes understanding, guarding our hearts and minds through Jesus Christ. To us, it seemed presumptuous to tell God what to do. We make the request; God makes the decision. We needed to line up our requests with the will of the Creator.

A week before Eva died, one of our friends, a very sincere Christian, came by and said that as she was praying for Eva, the Lord clearly revealed to her that Eva could choose to live or die. If she chose life, she would need to endure some pain, but she could live.

A letter arrived at the same time from a precious friend, telling us that in prayer the Lord gave this person assurance that God would honor her prayer of faith and heal Eva.

What were we to do with these developments? Eva was getting weaker and weaker. Our response was to turn to the Bible:

> "If you abide in Me,
> and My words abide in you,
> you will ask what you desire,
> and it shall be done for you."
>
> JOHN 15:7

"If you ask anything in My name,
I will do it.
If you love Me,
keep My commandments."

JOHN 14:14–15

The effective, fervent prayer
of a righteous man avails much.

JAMES 5:16

Building yourselves up on your most holy faith,
praying in the Holy Spirit.

JUDE 20

The eyes of the LORD are on the righteous,
and His ears are open to their prayers.

1 PETER 3:12

The Bible tells us that effective praying implies familiarity with the commandments, obedience, and fervent, righteous walking in the Spirit by faith. That is difficult to measure up to. Eva and I decided that as best we could tell, we qualified to approach the Lord once more. We could not honestly say any more than what we had already said. Our prayer was that we agreed with our friends that Eva could live, but we wanted God's will.

Eva died.

The Evidence of Prayer in Our Lives

During the time Eva struggled with cancer, another crisis was developing. I was involved in a real estate investment with a group of Christians. We united in prayer for the success of this venture. Without getting into the details, suffice it to say that the project was not doing well. The project went belly up and with it a great deal of my money.

What can you say? The conclusion I came to is contained in a Bible verse:

> **As the heavens are higher than the earth,**
> **So are My ways higher than your ways,**
> **and My thoughts than your thoughts.**
> ISAIAH 55:9

There were many, many people who were united in requesting that Eva should live. There were many people praying for the success of that business venture.

One must conclude that none of us were thinking God's thoughts, nor did our wishes fit with His ways. This requires all of us to search our hearts daily to be sure we qualify to speak in Jesus' name.

Knute Larson wrote on prayer, using a good visual aid that I feel helps explain our interaction with God in the area of prayer:

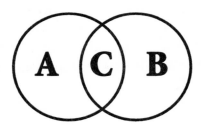

> **"If you ask anything in my name,**
> **I will do it."**
> JOHN 14:14

Area A is prayers we pray that are not answered, possibly because we ask selfishly.

> **You ask and do not receive,**
> **because you ask amiss,**
> **that you may spend it on your pleasures.**
> JAMES 4:3

Area B is where there are blessings or things God would do for us if we just asked. The Bible tells us why we don't have them:

> **Yet you do not have**
> **because you do not ask.**
> JAMES 4:2

Intersection C shows answered prayers in line with God's will.[2]

I can recall some glib prayers that I have prayed, such as asking God to help me keep my priorities in order or to help me place my family and the things of this world in proper perspective. I've asked God to use my life and all that I have for His glory. If I expected any answers, I didn't expect the ones I received. But death and financial loss did get my attention. And my experience with prayer over the years has grown to recognize peace, the peace only God gives.

Rejoice Always

The key to joyful, peaceful, thankful living is to plan your day, put your trust in God, walk in the Spirit, and watch how the day turns out.

Rejoice always,
pray without ceasing,
in everything give thanks;
for this is the will of God in Christ Jesus for you.

1 THESSALONIANS 5:16–18

Many years ago, I renewed a commitment to serve the Lord as my top priority. I was reading Psalm 1 and the first word, *blessed*, caught my attention. What does that mean? The concordances and dictionaries that I consulted said that blessed means "cheerful, calmly happy, or well off." I knew I was a candidate for that. Verse 2 gave one characteristic of this blessed person:

But his delight is in the law of the LORD,
And in His law he meditates day and night.

PSALMS 1:2

That struck me as a very tall order in that the law of the Lord is contained in a very thick book called the Bible. And how does one meditate day and night?

At the time, it was basketball season and I loved basketball. I read about the game; I watched it, talked about it, and followed the careers of certain players. Basketball was well ingrained in the background of my thinking.

It was also very satisfying to play the game in my younger days. I memorized all the rules of basketball because I couldn't play successfully if they were not part of my subconscious thinking. I didn't have time in the middle of a game to say, "Now, what was that rule about standing in the key too long?"

Living is like that also. If we wait until the actual event, God's laws governing that situation in life will not be part of our background thinking and we will often end up making a wrong decision. We need to be ready with God's law in our minds so we don't end up with regrets after the fact. If the law is to be in the background of our thinking, we must first of all have portions of it in our minds.

Since memorizing is not one of my strengths, I looked for an easy verse to get started with.

Rejoice always.
1 THESSALONIANS 5:16

My goal was to spend two weeks with this verse in the background of my thinking. This meant that "joy, delight, great gladness, emotion of keen or lively pleasure arising from present or expected good" needed to be in me always.

Always? These were my first responses: You've got to be kidding. Who wants to be that joyful? Should anyone be that joyful? Is it even appropriate? What about a death in the family? Discovery that a child is on drugs? Your partner is in an adulterous relationship? Job loss? Investment wiped out? Addressed rudely? Injured in an accident? Neglected or criticized? Beaten or abused?

You can add to this list. Life doesn't happen the way you want it to.

While thinking about this verse over a period of two weeks, I did not succeed once in rejoicing for a full twenty-four-hour period. One day during this period, I was disgusted and dreading the day *even before* I got out of bed. (Have you ever awakened in the morning saying, "Oh, no, I woke up! Must I get out of bed?")

Can one enjoy facing a crisis? I've often thought that joy is on the other side of a difficult problem and that joy only comes with a solution. This verse suggested, however, that one can joyfully work toward a solution.

I concluded that this is not humanly possible. To rejoice always requires a miracle: not just an ordinary one, but a full-blown, supernatural miracle.

The Bible says that joy is a fruit of the Spirit of God (Gal. 5:22). This is a condition of the heart that occurs at any given time when one consciously recognizes the impossibility of human achievement of joy, and as an act of the will, yields to the joy of the *Lord*. The miracle then follows.

My friend, Sue, lived in Nairobi, East Africa, when she received word that her brother had died suddenly. She decided to go to California to be with her sister-in-law and attend a memorial service for him. The trip from Nairobi to Los Angeles was a long, demanding journey, and she realized that if she ever needed peace and joy, it was now.

As she started out on her long journey, she prayed for the fruit of the Spirit, peace and joy, to be her companion.

It was an uneventful trip until she arrived in Dallas. The flight from Dallas to Los Angeles was overbooked and she found herself on the waiting list. One by one names were called and she watched the passengers go on board.

It occurred to her that she might not get on this flight which meant she would miss the memorial service. Because she had prayed that she would get there in time for the service, it never occurred to her that she would miss it after traveling ten thousand miles. The thought crept into her mind that if she were to enjoy this moment, it would have to be in Dallas, wait-listed, and likely to miss the plane.

In fact, she did miss the plane. Only a miracle could give her joy in her heart in this situation, and she needed it now more than ever. At this point she could enjoy making the best of the predicament, or she could be unhappy and bitter. Either way, she was stuck in Dallas.

She chose to ask the Lord to fill her with His joy and God responded to her request. She has the same option every day. We all do.

Pray without Ceasing

Many people have never experienced the fun of turning everything over to God and watching Him control the situation.

The second verse I chose to work on was a bit more difficult—three words:

Pray without ceasing.
1 THESSALONIANS 5:17

A friend was driving me to the Atlanta airport. I was sharing with him my experience with 1 Thessalonians 5:16 and 17: "Rejoice always. Pray without ceasing." It was 4:00 P.M. and until then I had enjoyed the day. It had turned out as I had prayed.

We arrived at the airport early, so we sat in the car and talked a while. I said good-bye to my friend, entered the airport, and presented my ticket to the attendant at the desk. My destination was Asheville, where I was to speak at a nearby conference center that night. The attendant informed me that the flight had just left, and there were no more flights to Asheville until morning. I was stunned. My watch said there was plenty of time . . . my watch had stopped!

I quickly called the center in Asheville and told them what had happened. They had already dispatched a driver to drive sixty miles to pick me up: he would surely need some joy when he discovered I wasn't there. And as for me, I ended up praying and rejoicing all alone in a hotel room in Atlanta.

The evening alone was enjoyable. God gave me no clue as to why this happened. He was silent. Yet this was a rare day when I trusted and rejoiced all day.

The next morning I was at the airport bright and early. The plane was scheduled to arrive in time for me to easily make my speech in Asheville at 11:00 A.M. As I waited for the plane to load, I rehearsed my two Bible verses: "Rejoice always" and "Pray without ceasing." The plane was full and took off on time. It was only a half-hour flight, and soon we felt the plane head downward. What a good feeling. Then we felt the plane head up again. The speaker system came on: "This is the captain speaking. I regret to tell you that there is fog in Asheville; we are proceeding to land in Johnson City, Tennessee."

With that announcement, one could hear murmuring throughout the airplane. Most of the polite, nicely-dressed passengers became visibly unhappy. One well-groomed man bawled out the flight attendant because there was fog in Asheville.

I was rehearsing my verses and, strangely enough, contentedly watching God work. We landed in Johnson City. Our plane load of mostly disgusted passengers descended on a hapless ticket agent behind the counter who had just heard the bad news himself. One nice looking man banged his fist on the counter and moaned, "I want to get to Asheville."

As for me, I ran to a phone to call the center to tell them I wouldn't be there at 11:00 A.M. Unfortunately, the poor driver who went to meet me last night had already left for the Asheville airport. For the second time, the conference director had no speaker. The men at the conference center and the driver needed a good supply of trust and joy for this day also.

Meanwhile, Henry Brandt was rehearsing his verses: "Pray without ceasing" plus "Rejoice always." The ticket agent behind the counter looked harried. I felt sorry for him, so I went up to him and told him I was also a passenger. I encouraged him to process me last, and I would hover in the background and give him moral support. He looked at me as though I were drunk. What was a cheerful, relaxed, supportive person doing here?

It took an hour and a half for the agent to line up microbuses to transport us to Asheville. One by one the buses left with a load of disgruntled passengers. I was the only one left. He motioned me forward and said, "I'm sorry, I'm out of busses. But I do have a limousine out there and if you don't mind, I will send you to Asheville in it."

"I don't mind," I said. We went outside and there sat a long, black limousine. I sat in the back seat and motioned the chauffeur to proceed. Soon we caught up to the first bus. I waved happily as we passed.

That is the way it goes. Sometimes the day turns out as we had planned. Often it doesn't.

Prayer is just talking to God with our mouth or with our heart. How is it possible to pray without ceasing? Does this mean that one stops doing everything else and just continuously talks to God? What would you talk about? Do you ignore your family and friends? What about going to work and interacting with the people there? Going shopping? Going visiting? This verse surely can't mean what it says.

I can commit my day into God's hands. I can tell Him what I want to have happen. I can compare what happens with what my requests were. Then whatever happens, I can depend on a living God to look after me and I can trust Him to give me a day's supply of joy. Life may not always make sense, but I can always trust Him.

It is never dull talking with God because His plans are often different and better than ours:

> For My thoughts are not your thoughts,
> nor are your ways My ways," says the LORD.
> "For as the heavens are higher than the earth,
> So are My ways higher than your ways,
> and My thoughts than your thoughts.
>
> ISAIAH 55:8–9

The third verse I chose to work on had four words in it:

In everything give thanks.
1 THESSALONIANS 5:18

In everything? When the car won't start? Tire is flat? Your partner is fifteen minutes late? You are being ignored at home?

Give Thanks in Everything

I was asked to speak in Mombassa, a city on Kenya's Indian Ocean coast. My sponsor and his wife were named Justice and Jemima. They met me at the airport and seemed to glow with appreciation as we greeted each other. As we drove toward the hotel, he remarked that he was so thankful that a friend from another mission had loaned them this car. Justice's car was broken down and he could not afford to fix it.

He was pleased to tell me that a local congregation had made their church auditorium available. It was the best location in town, easily accessible from all directions. He added that very few people owned cars so they must get where they're going by bus.

About 150 people were already there. The mood of the people before the meeting was congenial and friendly. The host pastor received us gladly. Justice was elated at the turnout, for the response was beyond his expectations. The audience's reception of the material was positive. Many of them approached me to express their thanks for my coming. I might add that the meeting was from 5:00 P.M. to 6:30 P.M. so those in attendance could catch their buses before dark.

Outside, it was about 110 degrees. The humidity was as high as it could get. The church was located on as busy a corner as you could imagine and was also on a heavy truck route. When the signal light on the corner changed, the trucks revved up their engines to get going again. Cars tooted their horns frequently.

When the church was built ten years before, this was a quiet spot. The business area of the city grew in that direction, and now the church is surrounded by buildings, with the heavy traffic going by.

With no air-conditioning, all doors and windows were wide open to catch any movement of air that might relieve the intense heat and humidity. As I spoke to the people, the sweat poured down my face, into my eyes, and downward all over my body. The faces of people in the audience glistened with sweat. The church's public address system was turned as high as possible above the roar of the heavy traffic.

Next door was a Moslem temple. At 6:00 P.M. their public address system issued a call to prayer that could be heard for blocks. For a minute and a half, I had to compete with a Moslem call to prayer.

All this bedlam around us, and in this setting dozens of people expressed their thanks for a convenient location and a public address system that was louder than the traffic noise.

These people taught me that one can have a grateful, thankful heart in a setting where the body is struggling with heat and high humidity, where the eardrums are taxed to the limit trying to block out deafening noise and at the same time trying to listen to a speaker. Here, funds are limited and clothing is scarce. Medical attention is almost nonexistent; education hard to come by; money is precious. Housing is substandard according to our definition of substandard.

None of these conditions kept these people from turning their hearts God-ward and opening their ears to hear from Him. If they were to have hearts filled with gratitude and appreciation and thankfulness on this day, it had to be under present conditions. They could be discontentedly complaining about the present and dwell on what might have been or what could be in the future.

Surely these people would like a better lifestyle. They work toward improvement like anyone else. As I think about them, I am reminded of the words of Ruth Paxson: "A truly spirited Christian is a paradox in that he is always satisfied, yet ever seeking. He never thirsts, yet is always thirsting. He is perfectly content, yet always wanting more. He enjoys to the full what he possesses but knows there is more beyond and eagerly longs for it."[3]

The prayer of Reinhold Niebuhr has inspired many of us:

> *God, grant me the serenity*
> *To accept the things I cannot change,*
> *Courage to change the things I can,*
> *And wisdom to know the difference.*

I have had wealthy clients who are very discontent that they don't have more. Then there are people like my friends in Kenya who are thankful for very simple things. Is our response of trust in God constant, whether we are rich or poor? This is an excellent indicator of our walk with God.

I have seen in my own life that I need to stand with open hands before God. He can put into my hand or He can take out of my hand whatever He wants. This includes loved ones, finances, possessions, health, or anything. Sometimes it is painful, but I know He loves me and I can trust Him.

God loves us and wants our hearts to be satisfied with Him:

> **I know how to be abased,**
> **and I know how to abound.**
> **Everywhere and in all things**
> **I have learned both to be full and to be hungry,**
> **both to abound and to suffer need.**
> **I can do all things through Christ**
> **who strengthens me.**
>
> PHILIPPIANS 4:12–13

He also wants us to appreciate everything that He has given us now, even the difficulties, because they are there for a purpose that is for our good:

> **In everything give thanks;**
> **for this is the will of God**
> **in Christ Jesus for you.**
>
> 1 THESSALONIANS 5:18

CHAPTER 12

If You Don't Want To, You Aren't Going To

Thought Starter

Are your decisions in life made
on the basis of who you are trying to please?

◆

I beseech you therefore, brethren,
by the mercies of God,
that you present your bodies a living sacrifice,
holy, acceptable to God,
which is your reasonable service.
And do not be conformed to this world,
but be transformed by the renewing of your mind,
that you may prove what is
that good and acceptable and perfect will of God.
ROMANS 12:1–2

Now may the God of peace . . .
make you complete in every good work to do His will,
working in you what is well pleasing in His sight,
through Jesus Christ,
to whom be glory forever and ever.
HEBREWS 13:20–21

In my high school days we had a basketball coach whom I both appreciated and feared. When he was looking in my direction I always tried to be shooting a basket, which was the strong part of my game. When he walked toward me, however, I knew what was coming.

"Good shot, Brandt," he would say. "Now let me see you dribble."

That was the worst part of my game. I hated to dribble, but he forced me to do it. As a result I became a better player.

Every day during the Olympics, we hear and read about the athletes' years of sacrifice, hard work, and continuous training. There is daily talk about world record–holders. The standard of performance includes many comments on perfection: perfect physical condition, perfect weight, perfect skill and performance, perfect attitude, perfect concentration, perfect persistence in the face of competition or adversity, perfect teamwork if it is a team effort.

A few athletes achieve perfection; no one can maintain it. Yet athletes keep trying.

In the 1988 Olympics, Jackie Joyner-Kersee competed in the heptathalon, a two-day series of seven events for women.

She grew up on Piggot Avenue in St. Louis, across the street from a tavern, down the block from a pool hall, and around the corner from a playground.

"I knew at the age of nine that I could jump," she recalls. "That's when I started running and jumping off the porch."

A fireman's brigade of siblings used a potato chip bag to "borrow" sand from the playground and install a landing pit off the porch.

Nino Fennoy, a saintly coach of the kind these neighborhoods seem to inspire, steered her through a series of Junior Olympic championships and a busy career of basketball and volleyball at Lincoln High. The girls basketball team went 62-2 during her last two years, and Jackie was All-State. She went on to U.C.L.A. on a basketball scholarship and was a star performer there, too.

In 1981, Mary, her mother, who was the determined disciplinarian with a willow switch, died at age thirty-eight after a one-day illness. "Her determination," Jackie says, "passed to me."

Working under a U.C.L.A. assistant track coach, Bob Kersee, Jackie headed toward the 1984 games. She won a silver medal. She married her coach in 1986 and with his help, she overwhelmed the international field with the only 7,000-point performances (four of them) on record. In 1988, she took the gold medal. Jumping, she says, is like leaping for joy. "I don't know what it is about that extra second or inch." She always aches but never minds it. "To ask my body not to ache would be too much," she says.[1]

People helped her reach her goals in spite of the obstacles, but the desire, will, and drive had to come from her.

As I thought about this area of athletes and the Olympic atmosphere of striving for excellence, I recalled the struggles my wife and I experienced in the early years of our Christian life. We presented our bodies to God as a living sacrifice. We wanted our lives to be well-pleasing in God's sight. We didn't have the foggiest idea of what such a commitment meant or how to go about discovering "that good and acceptable and perfect will of God." There was no well-marked highway. There was no two-way direct communication with God. We had a lot to learn.

Our faith in God and in the Bible as the Word of God was very shaky. We needed some exercise so we could improve and perfect our faith and hope in God. We decided that we needed to study the Bible first of all. Then we needed to test it against life. We also needed some teachers and coaches to help us along the way. But the desire and will to study, to improve, had to come from us.

A young pastor, Dick Wilkenson, took an interest in us. He encouraged us to get a concordance and learn to use it. He said he would help us find biblical answers to our questions. We took his advice, and it proved to be one of the most helpful moves we made to get to know what "pleasing God" meant.

Dick introduced us to a biblical principle that disturbed us:

"Seek first the kingdom of God and His righteousness, and all these things shall be added to you."
MATTHEW 6:33

Up to this point in my life, my main preoccupation was in acquiring a home and the means to assure a comfortable, secure life. We had a new car, a new house, membership in a sailing club, a sailboat, access to a golf and tennis club. Even thinking about God was not a serious consideration. My pastor kept bringing up this verse and urging us to review our priorities.

Sunday was the best time for sailing and doing homework (I was taking some engineering courses at night). Golf or tennis took two or three evenings. Looking after the lawn, playing with the children, and visiting our families took up time. It seemed our world consisted of pleasing ourselves.

Training Requires Diligence

He kept asking us pesky questions in relation to that verse, such as: What are you doing with your time? What are you doing with your money? What are you studying in the Bible? Why weren't you in church on Sunday?

I had mixed feelings about him and his questions because I was embarrassed by the answers I had to give him.

Once, in exasperation, I told him to mind his own business. He said he was. As long as I came to his church, I was his business. He was my "coach."

Gradually, our focus changed from things to people. People appeared from nowhere asking for help with their problems, and we would invite them to come for dinner. We discovered that these dinner invitations were very expensive. Besides, we had very little background for helping people.

We started going to church regularly on Sundays. Our sailboat, golf clubs, and tennis racquets got less and less use.

For two years, 1942 to 1944, Eva and I struggled with that verse. What should come first in the use of our time, talents, and treasure? Both of us had a growing desire to know more about the Bible and to be of service to other people. Our thoughts went so far as to consider going back to college for a few years to study the Bible.

We reasoned that if the Bible contained the most important information in the world, we should know more about it.

Finally, my wife and I decided to test that verse. I compiled a financial statement that included everything we owned in the world. Then my wife and I sat down at the kitchen table and had an imaginary meeting with God. Eva and I showed God what we were worth and told Him we were prepared to risk it all in order to test this verse. We admitted that our minds were filled with doubts, but by faith we would try to obey God as a first priority. We reminded God that we were interested in the whole verse.

We told the young pastor about the step that we took and we were considering returning to college. What did he think? He replied that this was a serious matter. I had a wife and two children, a one-year-old and a three-year-old. I was just getting a good start in the engineering field. He could not advise us one way or another. He said we would need to take a step of faith, and one test would be that we should have peace about such a move.

We had to admit that the whole idea scared us, and we were very uneasy about such thoughts. Our minds were filled with doubt, but we did want to obey God as a top priority. We asked God to give us some sign that we were thinking straight. We were very young Christians and were just learning what it meant to walk by faith, and faith doesn't require signs in order to move ahead.

We shared our thoughts with our parents and some trusted friends. They were all in agreement that we would be making a serious blunder.

The desire to know more about the Bible persisted. Should we abide by the judgment of our parents and friends? We asked God that question. His answer?

Silence.

Our pastor referred us to two Bible verses for our consideration as backup for his previous advice. We had to exercise our faith and yet be at ease about any move we made.

> Without faith it is impossible to please Him,
> for he who comes to God must believe that He is,
> and that He is a rewarder
> of those who diligently seek Him.
> HEBREWS 11:6

> May the God of hope fill you
> with all joy and peace in believing,
> that you may abound in hope
> by the power of the Holy Spirit.
> ROMANS 15:13

This verse in Romans is one of my favorite Bible verses and if I understand it correctly, hope is entwined with joy and peace. These are the fruit of the Spirit. So we can hope or expect to handle the circumstances that come our way with an inner calm, free from agitation, untroubled by conflict or commotion.

The more we thought about expanding our biblical knowledge and serving people, the better we liked the idea, and we became excited about going back to college. To do this meant that we had to sell the house and the boat. We could then finance two to three years of study time.

Again we asked God for a sign. His answer?

Silence.

Running the Race

We decided to sell the house and the boat. All of our friends just shook their heads at our folly. Even the young pastor expressed doubts about our decision. It was 1944. As it turned out, we spent three of perhaps the most important years of our lives at Houghton College. It was there that we met many hundreds of fellow Christians who were also exercising their faith, studying to understand the Bible, and learning to live joyful, peaceful lives.

This experience sounds like a contradiction. On the one hand, my wife and I benefited greatly from the teachers, pastors, and friends we made along the way. On the other hand, there were times when we had to go it alone by faith in a loving God.

The Olympic atmosphere is the same. The athletes strive diligently to develop minds and bodies. Preparation involves following the advice of teachers and coaches. But while the race is run, the athlete must go it alone and draw on past training and experience. Hopefully, the time of preparation will enable the athlete to perform better than ever before in the actual event. Everyone realizes that present performance is a compound of continuous preparation plus drawing on past experience. Even then, perfection is an elusive goal.

There is always a chance to start over when you fall on your face. The person who wants to improve works on developing and maintaining a wholesome personal life. A person needs some biblical principles and some teachers and coaches who will help him locate himself and guide him along the way. No one can maintain perfection, to be sure, but everyone can point toward perfection and work on getting closer.

When an athlete enters a contest that requires physical strength, he must have built up strength before the event. It's too late to start it when the contest begins. Practicing faith is also an exercise. It builds confidence in God just as physical exercise builds muscle. This faith in God must be built up before a crisis, just like muscles must be built up before an event.

We were in for a surprise.

It was in January 1947, when a professor at Houghton College challenged me to go on for a master's degree in clinical psychology. I prayed and told God that I would want the best training available if that was the direction we should go. I asked Him to allow me to go to one of three universities that had what I believed to be good programs: University of Michigan, University of Minnesota, and University of Chicago. I also reminded God that my financial resources were dwindling and I was trusting Him to show me what to do about it. All three universities turned me down. In asking God for an explanation, His answer?

Silence.

I had received several good job offers, but it seemed to me that it made more sense to continue my education. From January through August I made many attempts to get God's attention for some specific guidance. I yelled at Him and expressed my anger and disgust at what I perceived to be His lack of attention to my problems. I even threatened to turn my back on Him and to tell people how He had treated me as I pouted for a while. His answer?

Silence.

In August I moved my family to Detroit, my home town, and temporarily moved in with my folks. There was a new school in Detroit, Wayne State University, that met in a condemned high school building. Reluctantly, I contacted the head of the clinical psychology department. He looked at my transcripts and commented that he did not like the Bible courses listed there, but he finally said that I could study at Wayne on academic probation for the first year. When I paid my tuition, I had exactly one dime left to my name, a wife, and three children. I flipped the dime into the air with my thumb, caught it with the same hand and crossed the street to buy a Coke.

"That's what I get for putting my faith in You," I prayed. "I'm broke, on probation, and in a dump of a school." God's answer? You guessed it:

Silence.

One of the biblical principles that I had been depending on was that if we put the kingdom of God and His righteousness first, all these things will be added to us. To my mind, I had kept my end of the bargain. Right then it seemed to me that God had not kept His side of the deal.

My first class at Wayne State was in test administration. The professor paired us up in groups of two. We were to take a test and see which one of us could do it faster. My partner, Bill, was a dull, sleepy-looking person who didn't seem very bright. I beat him easily. I was getting more disgusted by the minute. He asked me my name and what I did. Reluctantly, I told him, "Nothing." Disinterested, I asked him the same questions. He said he was the head of the Psychology Department at General Motors Institute. I thought to myself, "Yea, yea, what a big liar. This guy couldn't head up sharpening the pencils at General Motors." He asked me, "Do you want a job?"

"Huh! Do I want a job?"

It turned out he *really was* what he said he was. In a matter of weeks I was teaching in the psychology department at General Motors Institute. In addition to a job, one of my benefits included a new Pontiac car, when cars after World War II were as scarce as hen's teeth. In addition, all my tuition was paid to work on a master's degree.

I told Bill, my new boss and angel, that all this was an answer to prayer. He replied, "The heck it is! I'm an atheist. I needed a teacher, and you're qualified."

God Is Faithful

After teaching there for six months, my boss asked me to prepare some courses in Marriage and the Family for General Motors engineers because the company realized that an engineer couldn't work at his best level if problems in his marriage and family were on his mind. He told me I could consult with any sources anywhere in the world. This assignment gave me instant credibility with people whom I contacted and the opportunity to learn from some world-class teachers. This was exactly what I had asked God to do for me. Some of these teachers with whom I came into contact during this project later opened doors for me to study for a Ph.D. degree at Cornell University. He knew better than I where to get the finest training.

Once more, I learned that God is faithful. We can trust Him. Although God is sometimes silent, that never means He is not there.

I also believe God let my bank account dwindle to nothing because I really did not trust Him. At the time I wouldn't admit, even to myself, that I didn't really trust God. He waited until I was broke before He stepped in. He let me know that He could replenish my funds in His way and in His time.

Again, I asked God why He didn't explain to me what He was doing. His answer?

Silence ... but things were happening during His silence.

This experience helped me put my faith in the power of God. Perfect faith? Perhaps a few people attain it; the rest of us can work toward it.

As I look back over the years, I see that developing a real faith in our living God is one of the most important pillars that has sustained me. The events of life raised many unanswered questions. God was silent over and over for long periods of time, even years, when I thought He should speak. There was sickness, death, financial problems, dishonesty, deception, and on and on. I wasn't exempt. When God was silent, I often looked to human wisdom or human sympathy, which were both readily available.

The Bible says:

> **All things work together for good**
> **to those who love God,**
> **to those who are called**
> **according to His purpose.**
> ROMANS 8:28

We rest in this hope as we yield our lives daily to God by faith and as we experience the Holy Spirit's control of our responses. If, for whatever reason, we turn away from a daily yielding of our hearts to the Holy Spirit, we begin to ask ourselves questions like these:

- ◆ Why me?
- ◆ Why am I being singled out?
- ◆ Is God punishing me?
- ◆ Is that what I get for trusting God?
- ◆ Is this fair?
- ◆ What's the use?
- ◆ Why doesn't anything turn out right?

These despairing statements and questions are like a warning light on the dashboard of a car. It's time to stop as quickly as possible and find out what went wrong.

The hopeful person will calmly wait to see how things turn out. This picture in the Bible of a hopeful person is entwined with faith, peace, and love:

> Therefore having been justified by faith,
> we have peace with God through our Lord Jesus Christ,
> through whom also we have access by faith
> into this grace in which we stand,
> and rejoice in hope of the glory of God.
> And not only that,
> but we also glory in tribulations,
> knowing that tribulation produces perseverance;
> and perseverance, character; and character, hope.
> Now hope does not disappoint,
> because the love of God has been poured out in our hearts
> by the Holy Spirit who was given to us.
> ROMANS 5:1–5

If we put together the Bible passages of Romans 5:1–5, Romans 15:13, and Hebrews 11:6, they tell us that walking with hope and faith while experiencing difficult times in life produces perseverance, character, love, joy, and peace.

But tough times do not always produce perseverance, character, and hope; it only happens when we put our faith in the Lord. Turning away from the Lord produces hopelessness, anxiety, worry, anger, and rebellion. If that is our position, we do not benefit from experience, we only suffer when we go through it alone.

My first attempts at helping people go back nearly fifty-four years to 1942. Since that time, I've listened to many stories of people's problems. Pain, death, financial loss, personal inner struggle, family struggles, interpersonal struggles: no matter what the problem was, each one was resolved sooner or later, one way or another.

The way a person approaches problems depends greatly on whether he is hopeful or hopeless and whether or not the person is familiar with the work of the Holy Spirit. It also depends on who you seek to please, and often our faith is illogical to bystanders in our world.

When a person is in the middle of a problem, it is usually a major issue to that person. I've watched people who are as frightened over a minor scratch as others undergoing major surgery. I watched someone create as much of a tense, anxious emergency over a missing dog as came from another person's son missing in combat. I watched someone become as uptight over buying a toaster as others over purchasing a house. I watched someone get as upset over losing a car key as did another person whose car was stolen.

Response to the trouble that comes our way on any day will reveal our spirit, not cause it. If we fail to respond by faith and hope, we can always start over again. No one is perfect. God understands us and deals with us where we are now. The Bible says:

> **"There is none righteous,
> no, not one."**
> Romans 3:10

We can't change our past failures, although God will forgive us of those sins if we ask Him. But all of us can let the Holy Spirit control our lives today and in the future. This hopeful opportunity can be a pleasant, stimulating experience. God has made us to improve our performance and to enjoy the process as we see His loving plans come together in His timing.

Getting Started in Biblical Foundations

Do you know that everyone can finish the race of life as a winner?

Do you not know that those who run in a race all run,
but one receives the prize?
Run in such a way that you may obtain it.
And everyone who competes for the prize
is temperate in all things.
Now they do it to obtain a perishable crown,
but we for an imperishable crown.
Therefore I run thus: not with uncertainty.
Thus I fight: not as one who beats the air.
But I discipline my body and bring it into subjection,
lest, when I have preached to others,
I myself should become disqualified.

1 CORINTHIANS 9:24–27

What we have covered in this book are lessons that focus on the beautiful and simple truth that God loves us and has provided a simple way to live an abundant and peaceful life. This is done by confessing our sins quickly and asking the Holy Spirit to control our lives. If you miss the simplicity of this truth, reading this book has been a waste of your time.

Seeing the lasting results in my own life and the lives of thousands of others over the last forty years has convinced me beyond any doubt that the Spirit-controlled Christian life is a miraculous experience. As long as I keep my sins confessed and ask the Holy Spirit to cleanse and fill me as often as necessary, the miracle continues.

Although I hesitate to use the word "magic" or miracle, the Holy Spirit does work miracles in our lives when we turn our lives over to God beyond anything we could do ourselves. Even now, after seeing so many lives changed over the years, the results of the Holy Spirit working in people's lives still constantly amaze me!

Over the years I have found several tools that have

helped me find a biblical basis for my faith and the change in my life.

There was a lot of changing to do. Some changes were instantaneous and final: the urge to drink and swear just left and never returned. Other changes were more gradual and inconsistent: unselfishness, a servant attitude, compassion, experiencing the fruit of the Spirit. Consistency in Bible study and prayer also ranged from eagerness to nothing at all.

Bible memorization and Bible meditation have been the most helpful activities that have sustained me. Researching topics in the Bible has been a close second. A serious effort to understand the Bible was inspired by a fellow engineer who wanted to know how I changed my behavior at work. The challenge of giving him an answer got me started researching biblical topics. My pastor suggested that I get a Bible concordance.

I picked a few words to look up just for practice. *Love* was used in at least 1000 verses. *Peace* was used in at least 700 verses. In the years to come, next to the Bible, a concordance proved to be the most helpful tool I ever used to discover what was in the Bible.

The first question on my mind: Why study the Bible? I opened the concordance to look up the word *Bible*. What a surprise! The word *Bible* is not used in the Bible. I quickly learned there were other words: *commandments, Word, Scripture, written Law, Word of God, teaching, precept.*

I discovered there are hundreds of verses in the Bible that describe the Bible. I looked them all up; this took several months. I am not suggesting that there is a short cut to knowing the Bible. In the process I received the answer to my question about the Bible. I discovered that the way to understand a topic is to find as many Bible verses as possible about the topic. The Bible is the best single commentary on itself.

As a beginning Bible researcher, some ideas developed as I went along:

- ◆ Looking up verses helped me become familiar with the books of the Bible.

- ◆ Some verses leap out at you, some don't.

- ◆ Take your time. When a verse stands out, take a few minutes to think about it.

- ◆ If you have a day when the verses are "dead," quit for the day.

- ◆ Some days I had only fifteen minutes to work, other days several hours. There is no hurry.

- ◆ I developed my own personal concordance of verses that were especially meaningful to me.

The process of writing or typing out these verses helped fix them in my mind.

I have researched many, many topics. I will list some of them: God's resources, prayer, love, guidance or God's will, comfort and peace, power, sowing and reaping, sin, marriage, parenting, freedom, suffering.

You can add or subtract to such a list. As I attempted to learn more about the Bible, I worked on developing more than one topic at a time. I was catching on to the idea of meditating day and night.

I put topical headings on three-by-five cards and carried them around with me because I was learning that verses pertaining to my topics popped up in unexpected places. The most common place was the pastor's sermon. There were other places: at dinner, over the radio or TV, in a magazine article, in a book, or in newspaper articles.

One topic that has been especially valuable to me is "God knows the heart." I will use that topic to illustrate how my procedure developed.

GOD KNOWS THE HEART

2 Timothy 2:22	Hosea 9:16
1 Peter 3:4, 3:15	1 Thessalonians 2:4
Deuteronomy 4:28–31, 6:5	Isaiah 51:7
Matthew 18:35	Luke 8:15
Psalm 95:10	Psalm 38:8

On a three-by-five card I wrote "God knows the heart." When I heard a verse used or read on this subject, I wrote down the reference.

After accumulating a group of references, I transferred them to a loose-leaf notebook and made a brief description like a concordance. It looked like this:

God Knows the Heart

- 2 Timothy 2:22—Call on God out of a pure heart.
- 1 Peter 3:4—Hidden man of heart to be meek and quiet.
- 1 Peter 3:15—Sanctify God in heart.
- Deuteronomy 4:28–31—Find God when search with whole heart.
- Deuteronomy 6:5—keep word in heart.
- Matthew 18:35—Forgive from the heart.
- Psalm 95:10—Israelites erred in heart.
- 1 Thessalonians 2:4—God tries the heart.

- Isaiah 51:7—God's Law in heart removes fear.
- Luke 8:15—Nothing secret to God.
- Psalm 38:8—Roar because of a disquiet heart.

The list under this topic numbers over one hundred verses. Another step is to rearrange the references in the order they appear in the Bible.

There are books that have Bible verses already arranged for you. An example is the Thompson Chain Reference Bible. It's a wonderful Bible to use and to study; the topics are well worth the time.

I recommend this method to the one who is unfamiliar with the Bible. Most importantly, I learned to use the Bible and to fix the verses in my mind. The process of writing out a Bible reference with a one-sentence description of the verse helped me to fix the content in my mind. Later on, I would scan those one-liners as I added to the list. A quick review occasionally has been like a drink of cold water to a thirsty pilgrim.

Long ago I learned that I didn't need to argue with anyone about God, His plan, His peace, or His joy that is available to all of us. I cannot make choices for anyone other than myself. If someone wants to be miserable, that is their choice. I am not going to try to talk them out of their misery.

At this time I know that I am approaching the finish line of my race. And today, if I had a choice, I would not choose to go back and start life over again. I eagerly look forward to meeting Jesus and many good friends in heaven.

If I go before you, I would like to be holding the tape when you finish the race God has given *you* to run.

Now I live each day so that I am ready to cross my own finish line.

Additional Verses
That Define Sin

If you show partiality, you commit sin,
and are convicted by the law as transgressors.
JAMES 2:9

To him who knows to do good and does not do it,
to him it is sin.
JAMES 4:17

He who despises his neighbor sins,
but blessed is he who is kind to the needy.
PROVERBS 14:21 NIV

Rebellion is as the sin of witchcraft,
and stubbornness is as iniquity and idolatry.
1 SAMUEL 15:23

The wicked are like the tossing sea,
which cannot rest,
whose waves cast up mire and mud.
"There is no peace," says my God,
"for the wicked."
ISAIAH 57:20–21 NIV

There are six things the Lord hates,
seven that are detestable to Him:

1. Haughty eyes
2. A lying tongue
3. Hands that shed innocent blood
4. A heart that devises wicked schemes
5. Feet that are quick to rush into evil
6. A false witness who pours out lies
7. A man who stirs up dissension among brothers.

SEE PROVERBS 16–19

Whoever hates his brother is a murderer,
and you know that no murderer
has eternal life abiding in him.

1 JOHN 3:15

You have heard that it was said to those of old,
You shall not commit adultery.
But I say to you
that whoever looks at a woman
to lust for her
has already committed adultery with her
in his heart.

MATTHEW 5:27–28

We all, like sheep, have gone astray;
each of us has turned to his own way;
and the Lord has laid on him the iniquity of us all.

ISAIAH 53:6 NIV

If you have bitter envy and self-seeking in your hearts,
do not boast and lie against the truth.
This wisdom does not descend from above,
but is earthly, sensual, demonic.
For where envy and self-seeking exist,
confusion and every evil thing will be there.

JAMES 3:14–16

Your iniquities have separated
between you and your God,
and your sins have hid his face from you,
that he will not hear.

ISAIAH 59:1–2 KJV

She will bring forth a Son,
and you shall call His name Jesus,
for He will save His people from their sins.

MATTHEW 1:21

Blessed is he whose transgression is forgiven,
whose sins are covered.

PSALMS 32:1 KJV

NOTES

Chapter 2

1. *Fort Collins News* (Fort Collins, Colo.), 28 October 1989, 1E.

Chapter 3

1. Beninga and Spradley, "The Burnout of Almost Everyone," *Time,* 21 September 1981, 84.

2. S. I. McMillen, M.D., *None of These Diseases* (Waco, Tex.: Word, n.d.), 64–65.

Chapter 8

1. Billy Graham, *Till Armageddon* (Minneapolis, Minn.: Grason, 1981), 140.

2. Graham, 9–10.

3. Graham, 139.

Chapter 9

1. Jay Carty, *Counter Attack* (Portland, Oreg.: Multnomah, 1988), 59–63.

2. Frederick Buechner, *Wishful Thinking: A Theological ABC* (New York: Harper & Row, 1973).

3. P. T. Young, *Feelings and Emotions* (Englewood Cliffs, New Jersey: Prentice-Hall, 1975), 138.

4. Marilyn Manning and P. A. Haddock, "Temper Those Tantrums," *Sky,* July 1989, 100–105.

Chapter 10

1. "The Ship," author unknown, *Poems That Live Forever*, Hazel Felleman, ed. (Doubleday, 1965).

Chapter 11

1. Act 3, scene 3, line 97–99.

2. Knute Larson, *Chapel News*, The Chapel, 135 Fir Hill, Akron, OH 44304.

3. Ruth Paxson, *Wealth, Walk, Warfare of the Christian* (Old Tappan, NJ: Fleming Revell, 1939).

Chapter 12

1. *Time*, 19 September 1990, 49–50.

INDEX